CHANGING HOW WE LIVE

No man can make a greater mistake than he who did nothing because he himself could do a little.
                                                                Edmund Burke (1729-1797)

CHANGING HOW WE LIVE
Society from the bottom up

by Robert A. Hinde

*St. John's College
Cambridge*

SPOKESMAN

First published in 2011 by
Spokesman
Russell House, Bulwell Lane
Nottingham NG6 0BT
England
Phone 0115 9708318 Fax 0115 9420433
e-mail elfeuro@compuserve.com
www.spokesmanbooks.com

Copyright © Robert A. Hinde 2011

All rights reserved. Except for the quotation of short passages for the purposes of criticism and review, no part of this publication may be reproduced, stored in a retrieval system or transmitted in any form or by means, electronic, mechanical, photocopying, recording or otherwise, without prior permission of the publishers.

British Library Cataloguing in Publication Data
A CIP catalogue record for this book is available from the British Library

ISBN 978 0 85124 806 6

Printed by The Russell Press Ltd., (www.russellpress.com)

CONTENTS

Introduction		5
Chapter 1	The Problem: Working from the Bottom up	7
Chapter 2	Morality and Religion	17
Chapter 3	The Genesis of Morality	29
Chapter 4	Where our Current Morality Fails	50
Chapter 5	Adjustments to Morality are Possible	67
Chapter 6	Limitations on Change	76
Chapter 7	Morality: Four Basic Issues	81
Chapter 8	Social Living: Rights and Responsibilities	88
Chapter 9	Social Structures	96
Chapter 10	Building on What We Have	110
Notes		122
References		125

Introduction

That there is much to be desired in the organisation of western societies is obvious enough. It is usually assumed that the solution to many of the problems lies in changes to our political, financial or legal systems. In this book I argue that the assumptions underlying those systems reflect and affect the assumptions underlying the everyday behaviour of citizens. To be more explicit, where individuals are primarily interested in their own welfare, they are likely to create political, financial and legal systems that encourage self-interest. Reciprocally, such systems will encourage self-interest amongst citizens. The morality accepted by the people will both influence and be influenced by the political, financial and legal systems of the society. I suggest, therefore, that changes to our political and financial systems will not be successful without complementary changes to our morality. In this book I describe the nature of the changes that will be necessary and show that we have the capacity to achieve them.

My aim has been to present the argument succinctly so that its logic can be assimilated readily. I have provided references to back up each stage of the argument, but I have deliberately not entered into matters that are peripheral to the main theme, such as whether or not God or gods exist, whether religion is adaptive, or the question of free will[7, 27, 41, 88, 115, 130]. I have not spent pages discussing what I mean by 'well-being', though a detailed discussion might be seen to demand it. I have referred to several disciplines in the humanities, but my aim is not to explore them in any depth, indeed that would not be within my competence, but to bring together issues pertinent to the present issue.

Morality is traditionally associated with religion, and I shall focus primarily on Christianity because of my greater familiarity with it, though I shall refer to other religions. Chapter 1 outlines the nature of the problem and emphasizes the necessity of working 'from the bottom up': changing individual morality is necessary for changes in the political/financial/legal systems. The next chapter discusses the relation of morality to religion, arguing that a societal religion is not essential for a societal morality. The genesis of morality is discussed in chapter 3: this involves the two problems of how morality evolved and how we acquire morality as individuals. Chapter 4 notes some problems in our current morality, and chapter 5 shows that change is possible. However we must be realistic: there are limitations on what is possible (chapter 6). Chapters 7-9 offer some general principles for a new approach. Chapter 10 argues that change will be possible if we build on propensities that are already in our nature and points the way to a new outlook on the world that might improve our society. In my view it could be much more than *might improve*, but that is up to you.

I am indebted to many colleagues with whom I have discussed these issues, and especially to Richard Wrangham, whose scathing criticisms on an earlier draft were enormously constructive, and to Simon Szreter, for advice on a number of social controversies. I would also like to thank Joan Stevenson-Hinde for her comments at varioius stages.

1

The Problem: Working from the Bottom up

Few would disagree with the view that our present society is not all that we would desire. In this book I argue that the solution to its problems must not be left solely with the politicians, economists, financiers or lawyers. It is equally a matter of how the man or woman in the street behaves. I point to some of the changes that are needed, and argue that achieving them, although difficult, is not impossible because we already possess the abilities to bring them about.

The present state

We do not need a financial crisis or riots on the streets to tell us that things are not going well in our society. That politicians, whom we elect to govern us, should ignore their election promises as soon as they are elected is bad enough: that some of them should lie and fiddle their expenses implies that naked self interest is at the centre of our society. Politicians in many so-called democratic countries are subject to powerful lobbies from non-governmental groups. Short-term national and commercial interests take precedence over the long-term ability of the planet to sustain us and lead to the depletion of natural resources and pollution, with irreparable consequences. Morality and pragmatism become indistinguishable in guiding the behaviour of many. Competitive capitalism, with its over-riding goal of profit, has widened the gap between the haves and the have-nots: some CEO's are paid well over 80 times the income of the lowest paid workers in their company. Tax evaders stash away their wealth in tax havens and thereby avoid the taxes they owe to society. Those who manipulate the financial markets can get many times the income of those who make a positive contribution to society: a successful financier can 'earn' tens of millions of pounds in a single year. The excessive competitiveness of the market-place has spread into everyday life: professional footballers do their best not just so that their side will win, but also to increase their value in the transfer market. A platinum skull covered in diamonds sells for £100 million and is called 'For the Love of God': no further evidence for decadence is needed.

The bottom line is competitive greed: so many are striving to get more than the next man. For the rich that means many times what he needs to live a decent life. What are we to make of a banker who got £63 million in a year, or of the CEO of a failing major bank who bargained for a £600,000 pension? They cannot possibly have needed so much money[149]. How can we have allowed ourselves to be drawn into this celebrity culture, where entrepreneurs can receive vast sums by exploiting a young woman who has been born with a pretty face? Surely there is something wrong with our values when a soldier who had lost both legs in a landmine explosion in Afghanistan is offered £152,000 compensation by the Ministry of Defence, while in the same week the retiring CEO of a failing company gets a pay-off of £3,000,000[98]? Is it surprising that there have been riots in the streets? Is this the sort of society we want?

In much of sub-Saharan Africa medical services, educational opportunities, even food and clean drinking water are unobtainable. Between one third and one half of the people in the world live in poverty, and that means not just insufficient food and water but often also the deadening belief that nothing will get better, ever. Lives are ruined by war. Natural disasters, drought, floods, forest fires, earthquakes, tsunamis cannot be ameliorated because emergency services are lacking. That is not to underestimate the devoted work of the NGO's: OXFAM, Medécin sans Frontières, Friends of the Earth, UN Agencies and many others do vital work, but their resources are always limited. Even the aid promised by the affluent countries is inadequate, tardy, and diluted by fingers that pick away at the pot before it gets to where it is needed. Financial crises notwithstanding, we in Europe and North America are very lucky.

Not everything is bad, and we must not inflate the bad by looking back at a non-existent Golden Age. But the rot is widespread, and it need not be so. No doubt the causal bases for our malaise are multiple, and include the growth of individualistic capitalism and the increasing wealth gap, as well as the increase in the scale of society. With the dispersal of kin, 'neighbours' are often strangers, and personal relationships are downplayed. The disruptive forces in society, and the results of human egoism multiplied by the powers of technological, commercial and governmental domination, seem to be becoming too powerful for community impulses to cope with[100]. Moral systems face special challenges today from the growth of technology. Sometimes, as with genetic engineering, the moral implications of new technologies, if any, are not immediately apparent. Sometimes, as with environmental issues and global warming, the moral implications are clear but run counter to the individual interests of many of those involved in controlling the technologies in question. So I am not saying that people are less 'moral' in any absolute sense than they used to be, but that the morality to which we subscribe may not be adequate for the modern world. And the problems do not come only from those at the top: the phone hacking journalists may be obeying their masters, but their intrusions into the private lives of politicians and celebrities are made to satisfy an apparently insatiable public demand for dirt.

Things can get better
That things are not as they should be is widely recognised, and there is no need to exemplify it further. The important question is 'How can we make things better?' What we must not do is sit on our hands and hope for the best.

So let us start by recognising that, in the West at least, there are signs of improvement, at least in some areas. Pockets of slavery still exist in some parts of the world, but major steps towards its elimination bore fruit nearly two centuries ago. Wars still break out, but it is increasingly seen that war is not only nearly always immoral but also a foolish way to try to settle disputes. Violence breeds violence, and in the West war is coming to be seen as a method of last resort for settling international disputes. In 1914 the outbreak of hostilities was cause for excitement and even rejoicing in Britain. According to contemporary accounts, people were cheering in the streets. In 1939 the general attitude was more accurately described as determined resignation. And when it came to the invasion of Iraq it is almost certain that the majority of UK citizens were against it and thousands demonstrated in Hyde Park and elsewhere. This change has been related to an increase in the positive value placed on human life: most western countries have abolished capital punishment, the USA being a regrettable exception. Again, while far too many live in poverty, at least society does not simply accept it and efforts are made to raise public awareness of the problem and to alleviate and abolish poverty. Early in the nineteenth century a pauper could get help only from his own parish, now poverty is a matter of national and even international concern.

So we must take courage from the fact that some improvement is occurring, at least in some contexts in the West, and do what we can to hasten the process. We must not sit back and leave it to others. The eighth deadly sin is resignation and hopelessness. Some will say that the problems are economic, others that they are political. Of course, both are right, but that still leaves many questions open. Why was this economic policy chosen and not that? Why this political system and not that?

Most attempts to mend our sick society involve attempts to amend our political or financial systems by manipulating taxes within the country or trade agreements internationally. There is a supposition, or perhaps just a hope, that, if we could get these right, people would behave better. But the relations of our political and social arrangements to how we behave and the values we hold are two-way: what we do and what we value affects the culture in which we live, and the culture affects how we behave and what we value. Taxation and trade agreements are made by human beings who bring their own values to the conference table. Over both national and international issues they argue for the group that they see themselves as representing – and that means the group whose values they share. Nationally, for instance, it may mean business or manufacturing, or the Trade Unions and the workers. Internationally it means their own country, or a dominant category within their country.

That there are many political scientists and economists who believe that progress towards a better world is possible is perhaps a cause for optimism[39, 143]. But theirs is a top-down approach. It assumes that the culture that pervades a society determines how individuals behave and what they value in that society. Though partially true, this is a blinkered view. There is a reciprocal effect: how people behave and what people value influences the culture including the political and economic systems in the society[84]. Influences run both ways, and if we are ever going to understand the complex web in which we live, we must consider not only the top-down effects but also the bottom-up ones. People are not intrinsically more greedy than they used to be, but their interaction with the systems that we have created is leading us in an undesirable direction. This is central for what follows.

The general issue is illustrated in Figure 1. The course of a short-term interaction between two individuals affects the nature of their relationship if they meet again on future occasions. Conversely, the nature of their relationship, as it builds up over time, affects the nature of the interactions between them. The quality of their relationship is affected by the group in which it is embedded, and conversely the nature of the group is affected by the nature of the

Figure 1

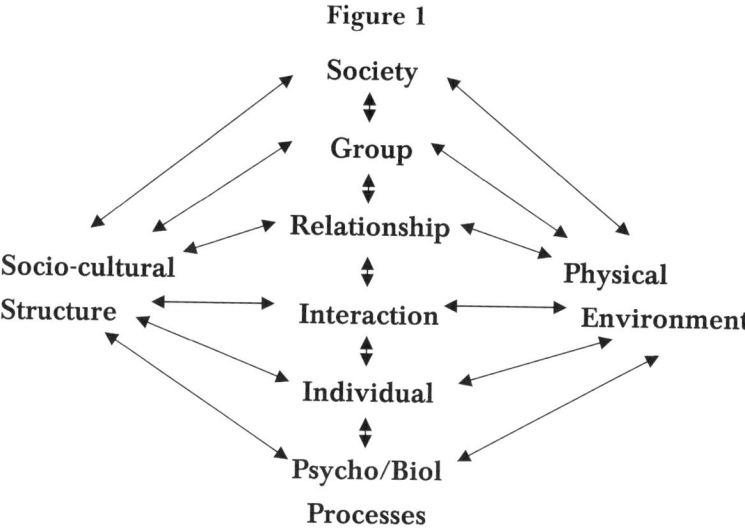

The dialectical relations between levels of social complexity. Each level affects and is affected by others, the socio-cultural structure with its beliefs, values and institutions, and the environment.

relationships within it. Behaviour at each of these levels is influenced by the values in the socio-cultural system, including the political and economic systems operating in the society in which the individuals live, and those values are themselves affected by the behaviour of the individuals concerned.

Consider, as an example, the acceptability of divorce. Before World War Two, divorce was considered disreputable. After the war, for a variety of reasons it became more frequent – for instance, men had been changed by their experiences in the military, women who had enjoyed independence had to give up their jobs to returning veterans, and so on. As divorce became more frequent it became less disreputable, and as it became less disreputable it became more common[84]. The change took place against a background of diversity and major changes in attitudes to sexuality. These in turn depended on wide individual differences in attitudes to marriage and a complex of changes in society including the availability of contraceptive techniques and in the ability of women to be self-supporting[147]. But the dialectic between what people were doing and what people were supposed to do operated throughout.

Figure 2

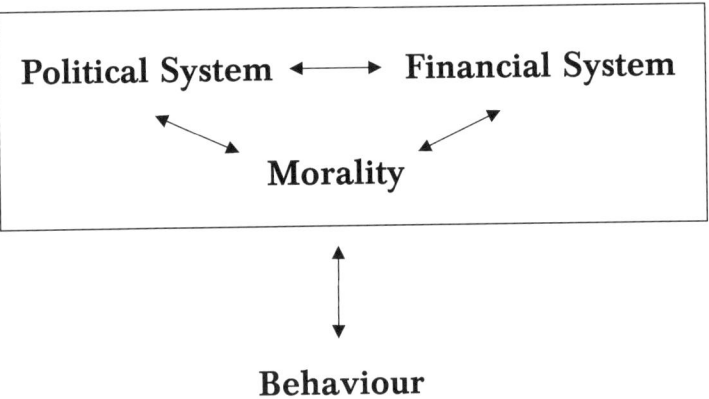

The dialectics central to the theme of this book.

I do not describe these two-way relations as feed-back because that too often implies a tendency to return to the original state. Instead the two-way effects can be referred to as 'dialectical' because each state can lead to change, each change to a new state. Figure 2 abstracts the dialectics that are central to the theme of this book. Embedded within the socio-cultural structure, the political and economic systems influence and are influenced by the morality and values that individuals hold, and these in turn influence and are influenced by their behaviour. The greed and selfishness that is so conspicuous in our societies not only is encouraged by our present economic and political systems, but also supports those systems. And they encourage further change likely to exacerbate the situation. Such dialectical relations operating within societies may have beneficial or harmful effects on the society. In this book I consider whether a greater understanding of and commitment to personal and social morality can complement and perhaps guide the political and economic approaches necessary for building a better world.

Realising that we must re-consider our morality is only the start. Consideration of the nature of our morality, of how we have come to hold the values we hold rather than any others, will help us to prioritize our goals. Except for a few at the top of our hierarchical societies, most of us would prefer a more equitable society, with power shared more evenly or at least more appropriately amongst individuals. We would prefer it because it would be 'fairer', but also because it would enable us to live without many (but not all) of the tensions prevalent in current societies. Early in human history such societies were usual, and a few such societies, though on a small scale, remain to the present day. The behavioural propensities that made those societies possible are still present in every one of us, but are no longer given the priority they deserve. I shall argue that that can change if we order our values correctly.

But it is not only a matter of ordering our priorities. As we shall see in chapter 3, humans are inherently selfish, but they are also inherently prosocial. At some level, we all want to help our fellows, we do not want a society where dog bites dog is the sole order of the day. That means diluting our desire to do the best for oneself with the aim of enhancing common well-being. That, of course, raises a host of problems: many pates have been bloodied in disputes over what is best for all. I shall leave that on one side with a reminder of the positive things that can happen when a community faces disaster. Every one has heard how mutual aid took over in the Blitz in Britain during World War Two; and the same is evident in the aftermath of the tsunami in Japan and in the 2011 riots in London.

Some will think that an approach that starts with morality is an inappropriate course for a scientist to take: there have been countless attempts to make the world a better place by influencing how people behave and what they value, and most have been by philosophers or theologians[46]. You may well ask whether a scientist has any right to intrude on this field? Philosophers who claim that science is concerned solely with what people do, and not with what they ought to do, are in my view out of date. Subjective judgements of right and wrong are made in the brain, and it is the scientist's business to understand them. Philosophers, it seems, are not wholly satisfied with the progress made in moral philosophy[165]; politicians, with their eyes on the electorate, are too inclined to seek short-term solutions; economists have been inclined to assume that all humans are simply greedy; lawyers tend to wake up only when change is overdue. Perhaps it will help if we can understand the bases of our morality, and the relations of our morality to how we actually behave. But for that natural science must be married to the humanities and, I am not ashamed to admit, to common sense.

For the sake of fellow scientists, I must make two reservations here. First, good science requires measurement and the testing of hypotheses. Many scientists would regard my fumbling in the darkness of ignorance as mushy hand-waving. They would say first that my science is diluted with too much common sense, and we all know how misleading common sense can be. To that I would say first that the problem of the world's malaise is of such immeasurable importance that a new attempt must be made. Second, I feel that the need at the moment is for a brief synthetic approach. That is always dangerous, because in attempting to be brief one inevitably skates over distinctions and problems of profound academic importance: my only excuse is that I have tried to keep my eye on the ball. Of course, I have been led into areas in which I am not expert; of course, a focus on morality will not be adequate by itself, but a bottom-up approach may help us to build the political, financial and legal systems that we need for more stable, peaceful and wholesome societies. At least we can make a start. I am not claiming to produce a morality that will suit everyone all the time in every situation; in fact I believe that such a code would be impossible to attain. And of course I do not claim that we can turn the world or even the country around in a year or two: we need a new view of the world, and we do not yet know exactly what form it should take. But we do have some idea.

Accelerating (or reversing) changes in morality
And, I would say, let those who laugh at the *naiveté* of the idea that fiddling with morality will help us have their laugh: when I was a young academic I was teased by five historians in my college who thought that the idea that an ornithologist (as I then was) could do any good was hilarious – 'We historians, we know that nothing will put the world to rights'. Such cynicism will get us nowhere, and fortunately not all historians are like that. And I fully acknowledge that it is impossible to write about the world's ills without being hypocritical, but that must just be accepted.

I shall argue that our moral values are not just givens, part of the world we live in: we create them as we go along. We must live with the contradiction between the near-necessity of regarding our moral values as absolute and immutable, and knowing that they must change with time and circumstance. We have to come to terms with the mutual influences between what we do and what we value on the one hand, and our culture and the political and economic systems we have developed on the other. But we need to understand our values as a first step. Of course we do not yet understand sufficiently well the immensely complex interplay between the biological, ecological, cultural and historical forces operating to be able to prescribe for particular situations. The discussion in this book is concerned with the general principles underlying moral codes, but an approach which draws on the natural and social sciences and on the humanities, and which indicates that moral systems must be based both in human nature (its 'good' aspects but taking into account also its 'bad' ones) and in the society's history and current situation, and must change to meet new situations, does at least provide a starting point, and perhaps the only possible starting point. From there we can see which aspects of our behaviour and values most need our attention. It will be possible for us to achieve a better world because the means are within our nature. Humans are too easily written off as just self-seeking: we have the psychological characteristics that could lead to fairer, more equitable and more satisfying societies.

In brief, assuming that all will agree that there is much to be done about the state of the world, the argument is as follows:

We must attempt to improve our way of living for the benefit of all.

Changes in our political, financial and legal systems are urgently needed, but there are dialectical (two-way) relations between them and our behaviour as individuals as guided by our moralities. We need to adjust our moral goals as well as, and in order to, improve our political and financial systems (chapter 1)

Morality has usually been associated with religion, but religion provides an insecure base for morality in the modern world (chapters 2 and 4).

The genesis of morality, both over evolution and in the development of individuals, can be understood in biological and psychological terms, without necessary reference to religion (chapter 3).

The priorities in our present morality have many defects, but it is not impossible to put these right. Specifically, we need to allow certain elements in our nature greater freedom to express themselves (Chapter 5). In general, this means that individuals must give greater priority to the well-being of the community in which they live, relative to their natural self-interest, than is the case at present. The task will be difficult and may take more than one generation (chapter 6).

Issues that need special attention can be specified (chapters 7-9). Most previous attempts to achieve the desirable changes have depended on placing politico/economic constraints on the behaviour of individuals and institutions. The argument presented here indicates that change must involve not only public policies and laws imposed from above, but also the grassroots of society itself. Changes are achievable because the propensities are inherent, though partially dormant, in our nature (chapter 10). This last point is the crux of the matter because so many attempts to change our social world have failed so often they are regarded with scepticism. That the necessary propensities are already present in our nature means that change is possible.

2

Morality and Religion

In advocating the need for an increased respect for morality, I am not saying that the old moral rules are all we need. Nor am I doubting their value. Rather I am suggesting that we must understand the nature of our current morality in order to see how we can move forward. This involves first understanding why morality is so often associated with religion. Second, it is necessary to understand how, given that morality is not necessarily the hand-maiden of religion, it evolved over evolutionary and historical time, and also how it is assimilated by individuals: these issues are sketched in chapter 3. Beyond that, we must try to understand why it is so frequently disregarded or inadequate (chapter 4). Only then will we be in a position to see if we can do better.

What is morality

I shall not be concerned with lists or classifications of sins or morality (see Notes 1 and 2), and shall use the term 'morality' very broadly. To label an act as 'wrong' we should be able to show that it has, had, or could have had bad consequences for the society or for individuals in the society. One can, of course, argue indefinitely about how to recognise when behaviour is 'bad': I will return to that issue briefly later (p. 52-53). Where the consequences for society or individual clash, the former would generally be given precedence. When Capt. Oates sacrificed himself by walking out into the blizzard believing that his incapacities would prevent Scott and his companions' return from their journey to the South Pole, we see it as a moral act. If an Inuit group sets off on a hazardous journey to find more favourable conditions, leaving an old person who would fatally handicap their progress to die alone, we do not like the idea but are forced to see it as the morally understandable course in the circumstances.

This example also serves to illustrate the great differences in morality to be found between cultures – differences that may stem from differences in their histories or environments. The severe conditions make it necessary for the Inuit group to move and inevitable that the old person would be an unacceptable obstacle to survival. Again, circumstances affect judgements of morality: the Inuit decision might well depend on just how incapacitated the old person is, and how severe the conditions for travelling. As I shall emphasize later, moral dictates must sometimes be flexible.

Within that broad concept of morality it is usual to distinguish 'moral transgressions' that concern the rights and welfare of others from 'convention transgressions' that structure social interactions within social systems and are mere local rules with no pretension to permanence, like the rule stating which side of the road you should drive on. Moral transgressions are those that harm others, physically or psychologically, or disrupt the harmonious functioning of society. They are regarded as more serious and are less modifiable than conventional transgressions, and are believed to involve a distinct conceptual domain[155]. This distinction between morality and conventions is supported by experimental evidence but leaves many ambiguities[84]. For instance, many of our religious precepts were probably introduced by priests to enhance their own positions or to mark believers as distinct from non-believers (p. 86). Is bowing towards the altar or to the Cross in Christian churches a moral act or a convention? Is it perceived differently by those who bow and those who do not? Some of those who make this gesture certainly feel that they *ought* to do it, but that means merely that, given the culture they live in, it makes them feel better to bow. Most Church of England clergy whom I have asked, while embarrassed to be asked, see it as a gesture of respect, but differ as to whether it is a moral requirement. Again, our cultural conventions of politeness serve to maintain an harmonious society, and for that reason might be regarded as moral requirements. In this book my focus is simply on what the individual is supposed to do, not do, or value, and I shall sometimes blur the distinction between morals and conventions.

However, within moral transgressions, I shall recognise another fuzzy distinction, that between Principles, which are probably present in all societies and without which individuals could hardly live in groups, and Precepts, which may be widespread but are not ubiquitous. Thus the assumption that mothers should look after their children, and the prohibition against killing a member of your own group, are almost certainly to be found in all cultures (though not observed by every member of every society). However, as with so many moral rules, there are let-outs in certain circumstances: infanticide is regarded as understandable in some places where many women are so impoverished that they stand no chance of rearing a baby successfully[129] and the execution of some criminals is normal practice in some societies. I shall suggest later that the Golden Rule of

Do-as-you-would-be-done-by, or some variant thereof, is fundamental in most societies, though again certain let-outs may be recognised. By contrast rules that people should stand up when the national anthem is played, or that children in school should salute the flag every morning, are likely to be specific to the culture. This distinction between Principles and Precepts also has blurred edges: for one thing, we cannot know that principles are ubiquitous across all societies because the data simply do not exist.

Relation of morality to religion

Every society needs rules, guidelines or values by which individuals run their lives, and moral codes have often been seen as initiated and maintained by divine authority. As will become apparent, my own view is that moral rules and values were the product of humans or of human societies to suit their own needs, and responsibility for morality was appropriated early on by priests or other religious specialists to support their own positions. As long ago as the early second millennium BCE Hammurabi, a ruler in Mesopotamia, claimed to be a purveyor of the will of the gods: the judgements he made were presented as interpretations of their will[23]. And even today, the pronouncements of the Pope are seen by many Catholics as having divine authority.

In Christianity and many other, but not all, world religions, morality has been seen as a component of religion, and it is therefore as well to examine that association before we go further. Because I was brought up as a Christian (though I now see myself as an atheistically inclined agnostic) the discussion that follows will focus primarily on so-called 'Christian morality'. Christianity consists of six elements: Beliefs that are outside time, like the 'Holy Trinity'; Narratives, like the Christian Gospels; Rituals, like the Mass; a Moral Code, epitomised by the Ten Commandments; Religious Experience; and a Social aspect[84, 88]. These elements are emphasized to different extents in other religions: for instance specific beliefs have been basic for many Christians ('Believe and be saved') but are much less important in Buddhism. The several elements mutually support each other[29]: thus the ritual of the Mass reflects the narrative of the Last Supper; and morality is conveyed in part through the narratives. The beliefs affect the integrity of the community in part because people are attracted to others who think in the same way as they do, and are especially attracted to others who share attitudes that are unverifiable[30]: religious beliefs are a prime example.

'Christian morality' has been fostered by the Christian churches, but in practice the basic principles, precepts and values by which practising Christians guide their lives did not originate with any particular religion. Similar values appear in all the world's scripted religions and are implicit in many others. True, in western societies the Christian churches have been principal purveyors of our morality down the centuries and deserve credit for that. And the moral behaviour of agnostics and atheists in our culture may have been influenced by its descent from a culture shaped by Christian forebears. But the claim that there is something uniquely Christian about our morality will not stand up.

Because language is so central to our existence, it has helped to think of morality in terms of a series of rules. Most Christians, Muslims and Jews see morality as ultimately derived from the Ten Commandments brought down on tablets of stone from Mt. Sinai by Moses, though its roots lie even earlier in the mists of antiquity. This basic morality was subsequently modified and extended by Jesus, the prophet Muhammad and others. Christian morality is empowered by the threat of punishment for misdemeanours and rewards in a future world for compliance. But moral rules must have evolved long before Moses, and there are a number of reasons why we should not take the association with the Christian churches as validating its content (see chapter 4). Taking advantage of the fact that their pronouncements were unverifiable, shamans, priests and other religious specialists could use the threat of adversity in this life, or the carrot and sticks of Heaven and Hell, or status in a later life, to support the necessity of good behaviour and to maintain the status quo. And they could secure their own positions by including respect for the deity and thereby for themselves as necessary components of a good society. While the churches have been active in promoting morality, that is not the same as saying that religion is the source of morality, nor is it a reason for accepting the validity of the morality they purvey. In chapter 3 I argue that prosocial behaviour and morality probably originally evolved in the context of inter-group competition and develops in each individual as a product of dialectical relations between human nature as it has changed over time, what people do and what they are supposed to do.

The status of Christian belief
For many, belief in Christian dogma has been the essential element in being a Christian. Recently, Dawkins[41], Dennett[42], Hitchens[92] and

others have emphasized that the stories in the Christian Bible, if taken literally, are untenable. You cannot feed five thousand on a loaf and a few fishes, the earth was not made in six days, and it is unbelievable that Jesus walked on water. For many of their readers the implication is clear: religion is not true and we would be better off without it. (It must be said that such critics of religious belief do not underestimate the importance of morality, and accept that it is unfortunate that morality and religious belief are linked in many people's minds). However, many Christians also take the view that the Biblical stories are not to be taken literally: for them 'I believe' does not mean 'I assert these propositions to be empirically correct' but 'I give my heart and my loyalty'[7, 8]. For instance, Braithwaite, a prominent Christian thinker, wrote:

> 'A man is not, I think, a professing Christian unless he proposes to live according to Christian moral principles and associates his intention with thinking of Christian stories; but he need not believe that the empirical propositions presented by the stories correspond to empirical fact.'[159]

On that view, Dawkins and other anti-theists (Note 3) are missing the point. Eagleton[53] sees atheistic fundamentalists as 'in some ways the inverted image of Christian ones'. Theists say 'of course' the religious myths are not to be taken literally, but perhaps they convey important truths. They can in fact be seen as parables. We use parables without a thought that they could be taken literally: Aesop's Fables are a classic example, and Bunyan's Pilgrim's Progress was read by many in the nineteenth century. Indeed morality is basic to much of the nineteenth century children's literature, and to some today. Today novelists attempt to throw light on one or other of the complex moral problems of the modern world. It would be possible to take the Bible as containing stories of moral value even though not literally true: whether the moral lessons that they purvey are applicable or suitable in the modern world is another issue. Some are, some are not.

Sophisticated theists argue that the 'God' they believe in is a more subtle concept than the anti-theists suppose. They suggest that God is not an entity and cannot be described, and faith is not belief in a deity but commitment to a life style and outlook that could make a difference. Armstrong[7] insists that theologians have held such sophisticated views of God and Christianity for at least two millennia. To most non-believers this seems like a cop-out, but the theists argue that God has to be experienced through behaviour or practice. This may involve consistent morality and a suppression of egoism: some find it to be facilitated by prayer, meditation, yoga and so on leading to a different form of consciousness. Practitioners often describe this as a 'higher' form of consciousness, but the validity of the adjective is questionable: agnostics would prefer just 'different'. However, the supposition is that religious practice can produce a mental state analogous to that produced by great music or art. 'Belief' to many modern Christians implies a sense of commitment but does not involve believing that the Biblical stories are literally true[4]. The big mistake, in the eyes of some theists, is to try to intellectualise belief. The power of participating in religion is that participation has an 'emotional punch'. In their view it is neither a matter of belief nor is it susceptible to discussion: they argue that the difficulties that seem to arise when it is suggested that religion can explain anything are because we simply do not have the appropriate words.

Believers may claim to have 'experienced God's presence'. The anti-theist is seldom justified in denying that another person had a certain *experience*, or in suggesting that the *experience* was not real, but that is quite another matter from saying that the experience proves the *existence* of spirits or God or any other entity[49]. I have adopted a similar approach in trying to account for religious experience: the words that people use to describe aesthetic experience are similar to those used to describe religious experience, and the content of religious experience depends on what the individual has been taught: Christians have visions of Jesus or the Virgin Mary, not Buddha or Muhammad[84]. Many people feel different after attending a church service or hearing the Hallelujah chorus, and that is a fact that cannot be denied, but neither religious nor aesthetic experience proves that any outside agent was involved[139].

The beneficial consequences that religious belief has for some are advanced by theists to account for the places where a rational understanding of religious belief seems to fail. In the past, events that were otherwise inexplicable were ascribed to a deity[88]. Armstrong claims that religious experience helps us to come to terms with guilt and aggression, and is a source of compassion. Others claim associations between religiosity and 'well-being'[74, 104] or that religion gives meaning to the world: this, I take it, refers to a coherent framework for interpreting the world that gives the individual a reason for behaving as he/she does. There are many millions of believers in one religion or another all over the world and it is self evident that religion does provide meaning for many people, and it does comfort many. In a BBC programme in which the families of soldiers killed in Iraq were interviewed, a number said 'He is up there', pointing upwards, or 'I shall see him soon'. When my brother died of wounds in World War Two my mother was comforted in a similar way by her religious faith[85]. These are facts that scientists must not ignore, but they do not show that religious stories are 'true'. 'Meaning' may be found in other ways – for instance in loving human relationships, in serving others, or in the beauty and mystery of the natural world.

Many claim that any beneficial consequences of religion are outweighed by its deleterious ones. The very fact that it causes religious teachers to induce beliefs that are factually incorrect is surely undesirable. More important are its social consequences. Armstrong can claim that religion helps us to come to terms with guilt and aggression, but it is equally true that religious beliefs can cause guilt and aggression. The list of wars that have been caused or fostered by differences in religious belief is a very long one. Such differences may be responsible for small imagined insults escalating into major wars[9]. It is fundamentalist religious belief that is responsible for most of the undesirable consequences of religious observance. Dawkins and his colleagues are certainly right over that. In 2011 a fundamentalist Christian preacher in the USA burnt a copy of the Koran: this was publicised by the President of Afghanistan, condemned by fundamentalist imams and resulted in the slaughter of UN personnel by fundamentalist Muslims.

In response to assertions that the Biblical stories are not 'true', many theists accept that the stories cannot be taken at face value, but reply that we can never know 'ultimate reality'; hence the need for 'faith'. Religious understanding accumulates and we are far from having acquired complete understanding. The existence of evil is explained on the view that it is God's will sent to try us, or to provide scope for free will. The diversity of religions is explained by supposing that each acknowledges sacred power in its own way. In their view, the narratives in holy books were never intended as truth, but as parables conveying a message to us. Such additional *ad hoc* assumptions are impossible to disprove, but deeply unsatisfying to rational minds that seek for coherence in their perceived world.

There is plenty of evidence that our tendency to ascribe unexplained events to anthropomorphic agents is adaptive and part of human nature[28, 70]. Furthermore, gods are not totally unbelievable entities, but combine human properties (e.g. they listen, punish, can be pleased or angry) with improbable ones (e.g. they are able to be in different places at once, they can interfere in the world). The human characteristics help to make them believable, the unbelievable ones make them interesting and worthy of attention[29, 16, 118]. This approach takes religious and aesthetic experience out of the realm of the mystical and presents it as an as yet not fully solved problem to the psychologist/neurologist.

We now know that deities are represented in two ways in the brain/mind[15, 16, 151]. When children are first told about God He is portrayed as a being who can intervene in the world to grant answers to prayers. In other words, He has some properties, like acting with intentions and acting as an agent, that the child already knows characterize animate beings. Other things follow from what the child already knows about animate or human beings, like He can get angry or He can be helpful. The child is also taught that God has improbable properties: He can be in many places at once, He knows everything, He is three Persons in One, and so on. These ideas are, of course, much more difficult for the child to understand, but are eventually assimilated. To put it in different words, incoming information about God is processed in two ways. The one leads to representations that are implicit, intuitive and inferentially rich while the other is conscious, explicit, analytical and abstract. The relative weight placed on these two forms of reasoning may influence attitudes to religion[117]. The theological concept is taught and is the one largely used when people talk about God, the intuitive one when an immediate response is required. The majority of those who call themselves Christians do have a very simple view of God as a person with familiar human-like characteristics who can intervene in the world. A literal view of the Bible and the prayers used in Christian services support such a view. The more sophisticated theists, using a more theological representation, respond to this common view of God with 'Of course, God is not really like that, he/she is like this ...', but there is little agreement as to the nature of 'this', and it is hard for a non-theist to grasp what is implied. These differences between theists and cynics lead to an apparently unsolvable dilemma. It remains unclear to non-theists why, if God is indescribable and not to be anthropomorphised, Christian worship continues to personify the deity and treat the myths as true: perhaps all that is just for the man-in-the-street? Is there a special appeal in animate or anthropomorphic entities on which one can focus hopes, trust, need for succour and so on, even when one knows that the entity on which one rests one's burdens exists only in the imagination? Is that why Fate, the Devil, God, Lady Luck or gremlins are so readily personified?

According to a study in the *NY Times* many people raised unaffiliated to a religion later join one, and most say they joined because their spiritual needs were not being met. I believe it to be a fact that many people do gain comfort and help from their religion, and this in spite of knowing that the stories to be found in the supposedly Holy Books are not literally true[89]. (As, indeed, can commitment to many other systems, even communism). I respect the testimony of avowed non-believers who find the Church to represent community, friendship, common humanity and compassion[110]. Religions do some people some good, but must not be given a special status allowing them to influence issues in the public arena by imparting prejudices such as homophobia or labelling contraception as immoral. So I am not among the anti-theists who argue that we should do what we can to discredit all religions. We should deny them the status they get when they are recognised as conveying ultimate wisdom or morality, or when they are seen as state religions, but give them credit where it is due, for instance for challenging materialism and consumerism in our society and respect them for what they do for some people *until* (but not I suggest after) we have something better to put in their place, something whose myths (if it has any) are understood as such even by the unsophisticated and which all can respect as valid in spite of the complexities of the world. In the meanwhile we must be constantly aware of the immense harm that differences in belief can do. Discovering what it is about religion that gives it its value to believers and makes it compelling to so many is an important task for the future.

My own view is that it does not matter too much whether some people believe that God exists or not: what matters is how they behave and the validity of their moral code. Given the uncertain status of Christian beliefs, one cannot accept Christian views about what behaviour is 'right' and what is 'wrong' as *necessarily* valid. That does not, however, deny the possibility that adopting a particular life style, suppressing egoism, praying, meditating and so on may bring positive benefits to some people.

The ubiquity of moral rules
Those who believe in the God of the Old Testament are likely to see morality as originating in the Ten Commandments and subsequently interpreted and extended by the priests and others. The first four Commandments refer to the fundamental beliefs and require belief in the deity and respect for those who propagate these beliefs. This may have been essential in differentiating the group from other groups. Jahweh was seen as the God of the Hebrews, different from and superior to the polytheistic gods of other tribes. The status of the priests or other religious specialists depended on their acceptance as purveyors of the group's religion, so one naturally suspects that the injunction to worship only one god was inserted by the priests themselves.

As we have seen, belief in the deity has a special function in integrating society. We all need support for our attitudes and beliefs, and therefore we are attracted to those with attitudes and beliefs similar to our own, and tend to match our own attitudes and beliefs with those whom we admire. Of special importance in the present context is that the attraction is more potent if the belief is unverifiable[30]. Thus it is important to leaders to encourage belief in gods whose existence or powers cannot be verified: the shared beliefs and rituals not only serve as a powerful integrating force for the group, but also validate the priests' position. Group integration is an important function of many other moral rules and conventions: every social entity, family, group, city, or nation, emphasizes the importance of duty to the in-group and has specific conventions about markers that indicate the boundaries of the group (see p. 35-36).

The remaining commandments refer to the behaviour of individuals or the relations between individuals within the group, and it is these with which we are primarily concerned. They require individuals to honour their parents and forbid killing, adultery, stealing, bearing false witness and coveting another's possessions, all of which are such as to foster good relations within the group. Many scholars argue that a correct interpretation implies that they were all meant to apply only to 'neighbours', that is to members of the same group or strangers living locally (Emerton, personal communication. See Note 4). It is not surprising that similar rules occur in most other cultures. The remaining Commandments also have parallels in other religions: to take examples from remote areas of the world, the Chinese Han record Buddha as listing ten 'evil things', killing, stealing, adultery, lying, duplicity, slander, lewd speech, envy, hatred and delusion[134]. And the Nuer regarded adultery, homicide and incest as against the spiritual order[58]. The Tibetan Book of the Dead (c.2000 BCE) implied that stealing, covetousness, killing, lying, adultery and sexual abuse were all proscribed[59]. However it is important to recognise that in the long run moral rules must fit with other aspects of the culture, which in turn is influenced by the environment (Figure 1). Although the problem of sexual jealousy is probably ubiquitous, proscription of adultery would carry a different meaning in societies in which marriage was not associated with exclusive sexual access. Thus in the Aché of Amazonia, a woman may have intercourse with many partners, thereby ensuring their subsequent help in rearing the child. The practice is maintained by the belief that the foetus needs to be sustained by repeated doses of semen[82].

Thinking in terms of the Ten Commandments suggests that morality should consist of a series of rules about things one should or should not do. That is a big mistake. In the first place, as we have seen, it is useful to distinguish between Principles, which are probably observed in all cultures, and Precepts, which have more limited generality. Some variant of the Golden Rule of Do-as-you-would-be-done-by, and the duty of parents to look after their children, and others that I shall mention later, are examples of Principles. These can be distinguished from precepts which are not necessarily ubiquitous, like the Commandment not to covet your neighbour's wife (see above). However, it is probably the case that most precepts have to be compatible with the Golden Rule. Thus Christian morality is also seen as proscribing the Seven Deadly Sins (pride, greed, envy, anger, lust, gluttony and sloth), all of which would be disruptive of the group (see Notes 1 and 2). These are mentioned only individually in the Bible, not as a list, but have been discussed by Christian teachers since the early days of Christianity. Some regard them as referring to attitudes rather than specific actions. They shade off into conventions that are specific to the culture in question, like whether you shake hands or embrace when you meet, or how many sides of the face it is usual to kiss on meeting.

Morality is too often conceptualised in terms of prohibitions rather than of what one should do. Unlike the Ten Commandments, the Beatitudes are mainly concerned with what you should do or whom you should respect – peacemakers, humility and so on. The Beatitudes and Jesus's teaching also shift the emphasis from what you should do to what you should value. We shall return to this issue in Chapter 7.

The rest of this book is concerned with how we can build a 'Godless Morality'. In his ground-breaking book with that title, Holloway[95] has described how a rational approach to morality would affect our approach to current problems – sexual relations, drugs, euthanasia, and so on (see p. 60) (see also Norman[118]). Here I argue that a new morality is within our reach if we build on previously undervalued aspects of human nature.

Summary
While acknowledging that the distinction is a fuzzy one, moral principles, to be found in (probably) all cultures, are distinguished from moral precepts (not pan-cultural).

Morality has long been associated with religion, but the association is not a necessary one.

So-called 'Christian morality' has many parallels in other cultures.

Many of the stories in the Bible are not acceptable to modern minds as literally true, but some hold that they carry meaning as myths. The appeal of theistic ideas is beginning to be understood in psychological terms. That the myths carry meaning or bring comfort to many is clear: the means by which they do so is a problem susceptible to psychological/physiological study. Discussion as to whether or not God or gods exist always ends in an impasse: it seems clear that it is not necessary to accept a theistic hypothesis.

3

The Genesis of Morality

Most of us do not think about where our moral values came from – perhaps because there is a cultural assumption, even amongst non-Christians, that they have a religious origin. The story of Moses coming down from Mount Sinai with the Ten Commandments inscribed on tablets of stone is deeply embedded in our culture. However there is growing evidence that morality almost certainly arose through the basic natural processes of evolution and cultural change. There are therefore no grounds for claiming that it has divine authority. This does not mean either that our moral principles can be disregarded, or that they are 'hard-wired' or 'instinctive'. This requires a digression, but since I and others have written about this elsewhere, it can be brief. Two inter-related issues must be considered: how morality evolved in the human species, and how morality is acquired by individual human beings.

The evolution of morality

We are beginning to understand the early genesis of morality, but progress has been slow until recently. Part of the difficulty arises from the difficulty of defining morality. Chimpanzees are closely related to our human ancestors, so some research workers are asking if they 'have morality'. If chimpanzees are much more prone to display aggression to members of other groups than they are to members of their own; if a dominant male chimpanzee in possession of a dead animal gives portions to other chimpanzees; if females behave 'respectfully' to the dominant male, are these to be regarded as evidence of morality in chimpanzees? Should we regard such evidence of possibly moral *behaviour* as evidence for *morality* in the abstract human sense? Such questions give rise to endless verbal jousting with no real resolution, so I am going to bypass the issue as irrelevant to our present concerns.

In any case, the precise criteria for moral behaviour or values may differ somewhat between cultures (p. 27). This is commonplace for anthropologists: what matters in an Inuit society may be different from what matters to pygmies living in a tropical forest. Even amongst industrial societies there may be considerable differences: for instance, some attention has been paid to broad comparisons between individualist (mostly western) societies, where the pursuit of individual goals is encouraged, and collectivist (mostly eastern) societies, where group norms and goals are emphasized[152].

Basic propensities

I shall take it as evident that humans can be selfishly assertive to each other and they can be prosocial. 'Selfish assertiveness' and 'Prosociality' are shorthands, each for a variety of types of behaviour. Selfish assertiveness includes aggression, selfishness, greed, and so on. Prosociality includes helping, cooperation, sharing, loving and related behaviour. The two categories are useful for heuristic purposes though clearly heterogeneous and, as we shall see later, the distinction breaks down if pressed too far: how far they represent separate mechanisms is an open issue[89].

Prosociality requires emphasis. With the media reporting all sorts of horrors and brutal acts, and with the memory of the Holocaust, Hiroshima and Nagasaki still with us, it is easy to believe that evil is inevitable. Slick statements like 'To put it bluntly, all life on earth is based on selfishness' requires to be carefully picked apart before it is misunderstood[101]. At the ultimate evolutionary level, which is where that statement was intended, it may be true (or have been true), but it is misleading when applied to the motivation of the behaviour of individuals. For most people a moment's reflection indicates that one receives or performs more prosocial acts every day than selfishly assertive ones. Furthermore, it is a matter of common observation that in both pre-industrial and industrial societies individuals cooperate with each other a great deal of the time. Why is it that the media seem to delight in reporting evil but are strangely silent over prosocial and cooperative behaviour? I shall give a speculative answer to that question later (p. 112), but here I want to emphasize that it is too easy to lose sight of the good side of human nature. Our societies could not exist if prosocial behaviour towards our fellow group members were not the norm. Selfishly assertive behaviour to others is not the norm, though the instances reported by the media are certainly attention-getting. So the first question is, how did these two propensities become part of human social behaviour?[19, 62]

It is easy enough to see how natural selection could induce selfish assertiveness: individuals who looked after their own interests would be more likely to reproduce successfully and would leave more offspring resembling themselves in the next generation. The real problem for biologists has been 'How did the propensity to be prosocial arise?' How could selection produce a tendency to help others who might be competitors for limited resources? Several mechanisms seem likely or possible. First, parental care is found in all mammals: each offspring carries genes from each of its parents, and only if the parent looks after its own young during development will the young survive and pass on the genes in their turn to their offspring. Thus parents enhance the perpetuation of their own genes by looking after their children: by honouring parents children both ensure that they receive parental care and may facilitate their parents' future reproduction. Respect for parents (and ancestors) is found probably in all societies, though the number of generations and the degree of relatedness for which respect is required varies. The demands of the young on the parents increase with age, and there comes a point at which the cost to the parent of satisfying the demands of the young exceed the long-term benefits on the parents' lifetime reproductive success[153]: it is then in the parents' interests to wean or reject their offspring.

Beyond that, it will also be of selective value for individuals to behave prosocially to other individuals who are genetically related to them, if the costs they incur in doing so (in terms of the negative effect on their own current and future descendents) are balanced by the positive effects on the reproductive potential of their relatives (Note 5). The biological value of behaving prosocially to kin will vary with the degree of genetic relatedness: for example, in two-parent families each parent contributes (on average) half of the offspring's genes, one quarter of a grandchild's, one quarter of a nephew's or niece's, one eighth of a cousin's, and so on[73].

However this genetic mechanism cannot account for why one should be kind to unrelated individuals. A second mechanism that has been suggested for the genesis of prosociality involves reciprocity: 'I'll do you a good turn if you will do one for me'[154]. This is of central importance in maintaining prosociality in human groups, but is unlikely to have been responsible for the evolution of prosociality in large groups[35]. Reciprocity in humans is discussed below.

The third mechanism arises from the fact that our ancestors lived in small groups consisting of one or a few families. These groups would have competed with each other to obtain scarce resources. Competition could involve cooperation within some groups in exploiting the limited resources more efficiently than other groups (for instance cooperation in killing large animals) or physical aggression (perhaps to steal women) directed to competing groups. It is reasonable to assume that members of groups in which the members cooperated with each other would be likely to be more successful than groups whose members were selfishly assertive to each other. Thus selection could promote prosociality towards other group members. Whether competition between groups could result in *genetic* selection for prosociality is controversial, for it is improbable that genetic selection could operate in that way in animals. But, because humans have greater cognitive abilities than any other species, a propensity for cooperation with other group members could be passed on to later generations by several forms of individual learning[27, 163]. It would be advantageous to individuals to belong to a group of appropriately prosocial individuals, and mathematical modelling has shown that, given certain conditions, cultural selection for predominantly prosocial groups could occur.

This does not mean that individuals in predominantly prosocial groups totally cease to be selfishly assertive to other group members: indeed what matters to each individual is that *others* should behave prosocially, not that he or she should: it could thus be to his/her advantage to punish group members who did not behave prosocially, while he would himself be open to punishment by others if he did not behave prosocially to them or did not take part in punishing offenders. Computer modelling shows that, in sizeable groups, strategies involving cooperation, punishing non-cooperators and punishing those who do not punish non-cooperators can be stable if the costs of being punished are large enough[26, 138]. Punishing also involves costs to the punisher, and the nature of the selection that ensures that the punisher could accept the costs of punishing is somewhat controversial, though several possibilities have been proposed[79, 79, 101, 138]. One suggestion, supported by modelling, is that the costs to the punisher are offset if the punisher acquires a good reputation and is therefore more likely to receive help in future interactions[128]. We shall see later that human groups still exist in which an egalitarian culture is maintained if inappropriate behaviour is suppressed by the 'righteous indignation' of other individuals (p. 68-71).

Religion is yet another route by which prosociality towards other group members could be promoted (Note 6). Religious leaders may require members of the group to cooperate, to behave prosocially to each other, even to share their possessions, either for their collective benefit or for less fortunate members of the group. Christianity has used the unverifiable, but incredibly powerful, costs and rewards of Hell or Heaven to ensure adherence to its demands. If the demands made by the religious group on its members, for instance in the form of time-consuming rituals, are demanding and therefore difficult to fake, the group is less subject to invasion by imposters and the members are therefore more willing to behave prosocially to each other[80, 138]. On this view, the evolution of prosociality to other group members is closely related to that of religion: a detailed proposal on how this could have happened is given by Atran & Henrich[10]. However there are limits: if the religious requirements are too great, the costs of belonging may exceed the gains[26, 99, 116].

The effectiveness of religiosity in inducing prosocial behaviour has been demonstrated experimentally. Subjects primed for religious concepts by a scrambled sentence task were more generous or cheated less in a subsequent test[123, 135]. Furthermore, subliminal religious primes (as compared with non-religious primes) increased the tendency of subjects to punish unfair behaviour at some cost to themselves, but only in those subjects who claimed to have previously donated to a religious organisation[114] (Note 7). In addition, those who receive from more fortunate individuals will be more likely to show loyalty to the group.

Thus it is no longer the case that the evolution of prosociality is impossible to account for in terms of selection. Several mechanisms are possible, each perhaps effective at different stages of the process of embedding the norm of prosociality in the constitution of individuals.

Note also that on the competition between groups hypothesis (see above) prosociality would be biologically advantageous only if directed towards other members of the same group: behaviour towards members of another group could involve unrestrained selfish assertiveness (Figure 3). With members of their own group, however, individuals should be selfishly assertive only in looking after their own interests, but prosocial and cooperative with other group members only where their interests lie in the integrity of the group. Thought experiments exemplify this. An example might be a lifeboat with a capacity for N people and N+1 wanting to get in. The individuals may differ in wealth, colour, achievements and so on. If you were already in the boat, which would you choose to reject? Not surprisingly, perhaps, subjects in both the USA and Taiwan chose to save kin over non-kin and friends over strangers[121]. By contrast, behaviour towards

Figure 3

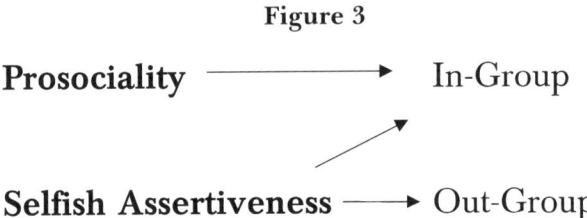

Whereas the propensities of prosociality and selfish assertiveness both influence behaviour to members of the in-group, selfish assertiveness is the important influence on behaviour to outsiders.

members of other groups would be selfishly assertive: hence xenophobia, the relative absence of prosociality and predominance of selfish assertiveness towards outsiders as compared with 'neighbours'.

The role of morality

The maintenance of an appropriate balance between prosociality and selfish assertiveness towards other group members is the main function of morality. Moral rules and values define and determine how people 'ought' to behave and what they 'should' value. If the balance tipped too far towards selfish assertiveness, the group would split apart. If it was too much in favour of prosociality, free-loaders could flourish. It is by promoting an appropriate balance between the two propensities that morality enhances the integrity of the group. This would have amounted to selection for a norm favouring prosociality towards other group members, but in the first instance a norm maintained in part by the assertiveness of individuals directed towards those who failed to observe the norm (see above). Initially each individual behaves prosocially or non-assertively towards other group members in part to avoid getting into trouble with his peers. This we can assume would become incorporated by selection into motivation for prosocial behaviour towards fellow group members so long as they are themselves behaving appropriately. This fits with the common occurrence of xenophobia – the relative absence of prosociality and predominance of selfish assertiveness towards outsiders as compared with 'neighbours'.

Equality vs hierarchy

Because chimpanzees and gorillas live in male-dominated groups, it is likely that our very early ancestors did likewise. However, we shall see later that many of the surviving hunter/gatherer groups lived in egalitarian societies in which there was an ethos of sharing and individual autonomy. The evidence suggests that there was an early trend towards egalitarianism in human groups lasting for something between tens of thousands and millions of years, and then male dominance re-asserted itself leading to the hierarchical structures of most modern groups[57]. Some egalitarian societies remain to this day, mostly living on the outskirts of modern hierarchical societies (e.g. the Inuit in the far north, pygmies in tropical forests, aborigines in Central Australia): I shall have more to say about them later (see chapter 5). Boehm stresses that the egalitarian ethos depended on shared intuitions, making constitutional conventions unnecessary[21].

In the egalitarian groups of hunter-gatherers, individuals who display exceptional skills might be allowed to lead in enterprises where that skill was of value to the group, but they take care not to be too self-assertive or bossy. Inequality probably arose as a result of the pattern of transmission of wealth across generations[25]. The emerging leaders supported their positions by force or by claiming divine support[21]. When the Hebrews were wandering in the desert, it was necessary for Moses and other leaders to convince them to remain loyal. The most effective means open to them must have been to insist (a) on certain traditions that marked them as different from other tribes; (b) that, unlike neighbouring groups, they had a single all-powerful god; and (c) that the leader had divine authority from that god for his pronouncements. Today, we retain a desire for a tension-reduced egalitarian society but are willing to follow leaders if we are convinced that doing so is good for the group and/or the individuals within it.

In-group versus out-group: In-group reciprocity

Given the probable sources of prosocial behaviour just discussed, individuals need means by which to distinguish members of their own group from outsiders. Initially, when populations were low and groups consisted at most of a few families, this could be a matter of familiarity, but then group-specific markers were developed: among the most powerful are differences in language, religion and group-specific symbols. Human groups isolated from each other soon develop dialect differences, and groups may come to differ in religion and morality. Sometimes a new religion, or a proposed change in an existing one, provides an incentive for group division, the departure of the Pilgrims to America being a classic example. In his study of the relations between missionary Christianity and endemic religions in Melanesia, Whitehouse[161] describes how the missionary religion was often characterised by tediously repetitive forms of worship. Groups, led by a charismatic leader, with new and more arousing forms of ritual that transmitted a coherent and plausible body of doctrine, might separate off.

As noted above, religious adherence, with the performance of religion-specific rituals, often requires much effort and so is difficult to fake. The stricter the religion, the more difficult it is to fake, and thus the more reliable the performance of its rituals as a marker of genuine religious and group loyalty. Furthermore, all groups, from football teams to nation states, tend to elaborate markers that distinguish their own group from others: these may involve differences in behavioural conventions, diet, dress, group symbols and so on. These become even more prominent in times of inter-group conflict.

Reciprocity

We have seen that reciprocity, the tendency to respond in like kind to the behaviour received, has been suggested as playing a part in the evolution of prosociality in animals, but the matter is controversial (p. 31). However, it is clear that reciprocity plays a major part in morality today: people are unlikely to behave prosocially to someone whom they expect to behave selfishly in return, and we shall see that the principle of reciprocity has been the source of diverse aspects of moral behaviour and values. Presumably this has been the result of cultural selection, though genetic changes may also have been involved.

A tendency to behave with reciprocity must have been present early on in human history: in non-industrial societies revenge, or the threat of revenge, seems to have been the principal, though not the only, way of maintaining order. If X steals Y's cow, he can expect not only Y but also Y's relatives to exact punishment[58]. The willingness for wronged parties to seek revenge would have acted as a powerful disincentive to anti-social behaviour in non-literate societies, and stories of revenge are found in the earliest human literature (e.g the legend of Gilgamesh). The extraordinary desire for revenge can be seen in to-day's law courts in the demand by victims or their relatives for the proper punishment of offenders: it is clear that revenge has become part of our heritage. However, a difficulty arises from the tendency of wronged parties to over-estimate the damage done to them, and thus pave the way for escalation. In the Nuer a dispute between two individuals could lead to war between family groups[58] (see also Atran[9]). This may have led to control of the punishment of offenders becoming centralised in the leader[1]. The settling of individual differences was presumably a different matter from restraining would-be leaders (see above) and must have been disregarded by other group members so long as it did not infringe group harmony.

More importantly, positive reciprocity is, and must always have been, the driving force in most human relationships. The most influential theories of human relationships in the modern world are the family of 'exchange theories', where the basic assumption is that those who behave prosocially expect prosocial behaviour in return, and conversely, those who injure you deserve to be injured. Many aspects of human behaviour involve processes of exchange, individuals incurring costs (in an everyday sense) in the expectation of future recompense. Thus one incurs costs in helping one's friend in the expectation that he would help oneself if the need should arise. The Golden Rule of do-as-you-would-be-done-to, or some variant thereof, could be adaptive: it is good to look after other people because then they will look after you when you are in need[83].

There are several reasons for thinking that reciprocity is basic to the moral code in virtually all societies:
 (i) Many moral rules are special cases of the Golden Rule. The Hebraic Commandments 6-10 are obvious examples – do not steal because you do not want your own possessions to be taken, and so on.
 (ii) At a gathering in Chicago in the early nineteen nineties at which all the major religions and many minor ones were represented, the Golden Rule was accepted as a Principle basic to moral codes[108].
 (iii) It is likely that the propensity to behave prosocially could not have become basic without some understanding of reciprocity.

Many consequences follow from the widespread importance of reciprocity in human relationships:
(a) Because a positive approach is more likely to be reciprocated with a positive reply than a negative one, it is better to at least appear to be a cooperative person if you want people to behave positively to you. Conversely, individuals are less likely to behave prosocially to someone they expect to behave selfishly in return or whom they

are unlikely to see again. The possibility of pretence is always present, though deception can often be detected[55].
(b) Reciprocation may be delayed. One possible difficulty with reciprocal exchanges is the time interval that may elapse between the initiation and reciprocation. If A gives something to B, how can he be sure that B will repay the debt? The longer the time interval, the greater the problem. If A is sure that B will play his part, we say that A trusts B. Trust that the recipient of a prosocial act will reciprocate if necessary is essential: trust is thus central to human relationships. In general, trust is more likely in relations between individuals who know each other, or even if they are just seen as members of the same group, than between total strangers. Trust increases with the length of acquaintance. A reputation for honesty is an important characteristic[157].

In the more heterogenous groups of modern societies trust in strangers who are similar merely in the sense of belonging to the same large group is limited. Communication and gossip within a group may be important in enhancing or diminishing the perceived trustworthiness of other group members[51]. Within a group communications that are otherwise pretty meaningless may serve to increase trust between those who have no other links. Everyday remarks such as 'Good morning', 'Nice day', and 'How are you' promote fellow feeling and trust. Such greetings are more common between strangers in the country than in the town.

In our materialistic society we must trust advertisers, experts, political leaders and many others[63, 105]. With the increasing complexity of modern societies trust in personal relationships is sometimes being replaced by contracts: even marrying couples are often advised to sign a contract to determine the disposal of their joint possessions in case of marital failure.
(c) In potentially long-term relationships it will be important for both parties to consider not only their own expected rewards and costs but also those of the partner: if the partner is not satisfied with what you do he/she may leave the relationship without reciprocating. Hence the importance of mutual understanding (p. 89).
(d) We learn from experience, becoming more trusting as we experience trust in others. We also become more discriminating, able to treat other individuals as more or less trustworthy. Trust in a close relationship may require self-revelation and thus some increase in vulnerability. Trust in modern societies depends on the

network of agents involved directly or indirectly in the transaction[40].

(e) Reciprocation need not be in the same currency: a craftsman uses his skill in the expectation of a monetary reward. Furthermore, the return may be symbolic: when a stranger does you a good turn he expects you at least to thank him in return. What matters may be not the actual return but the perceived outcome: in this way partners in a close relationship may make sacrifices for those whom they love. The route to successful exchange is often referred to as a variant of the 'Golden Rule' such as 'Do-to others-as-you-think-they-would-wish'.

(f) A basic issue in exchange is that the exchange should be seen to be 'fair'. Here, however there are many problems. For one thing, people use several criteria for fairness. Should the benefit received or expected by the initiator be equivalent to his costs? Or should the initiator expect a return as costly to the recipient as his initiation was to him, or according to their respective needs? Or is it a matter of entitlement: over some issues, individuals who are of high status, or have special qualifications, or are beautiful or rich, or have acquired 'celebrity' status, may expect more. And where there are several recipients, should they get equal shares, or a share according to their needs, or a share according to their own costs? Each will compare his share with those of others[96]. As there are no generally accepted scales for measuring needs or contributions, the participants may use different scales. Furthermore, the assessment of gain-minus-costs may involve predictions about an uncertain future[94].

(g) The sequelae of exchange may involve not only the two individuals involved, but also third parties. If an individual is seen by a third party to be a partner in a fair exchange, he/she may be seen as an honest person to deal with, and be chosen as a future exchange partner, by the looker-on. This 'indirect reciprocity' could have been an element in the evolution of prosociality[3].

Clearly, while exchange is basic to much of human morality, and to many of its aspects, such as trust, honesty and politeness, there is often ample scope for disagreement and conflict[84], and the notion of fairness is much more complex than is assumed by Hutton[98] and other political commentators.

What all this amounts to is that certain Principles, such as the duty of parental care, exchange and the Golden Rule of reciprocity are likely to be found at least by implication in all societies. They were probably implicitly understood at first, and later formulated into rules.

Criteria

It is generally held that science can have little to say about what is good or bad: it is concerned with what people do, not with what they are supposed to do. So far I have evaded the question of what is good and what is bad, and just assumed that we all know. However we have seen that prosociality probably evolved in the context of inter-group competition (p. 31-32). This hypothesis fits many of the facts about moral behaviour, such as the difference between what is seen as appropriate to in-group and to out-group members. It implies that the integrity of the group is an important issue. At the same time, natural selection acts on individuals to favour those who look after their own interests and therefore do better in competition with others in their group. I have suggested that morality serves to maintain an appropriate balance between prosocial and anti-social or competitive behaviour to other group members. As a tentative suggestion, this suggests that society's ills stem, in part, from individuals placing too much emphasis on their own good and not enough on their relationships with others and the good of the community as a whole. I shall return to this issue later.

Later evolution

We have seen that human groups must have developed some common view about what was and what was not appropriate behaviour, and individuals who behaved inappropriately were paid back in similar terms. Indeed in many pre-industrial societies order was maintained by threat of revenge. Individuals were deterred from stealing their neighbour's weapons or seducing another's spouse by such a threat of revenge. The revenge could be administered not only by the wronged individual but also by his/her relatives and, since the parties involved would be likely to have differing views about what was appropriate recompense, escalation was always probable.

Inevitably, given the inherent self-assertiveness of individuals, as groups became larger, leaders emerged[1, 25]: order could then be maintained by the leader becoming responsible for enforcing appropriate behaviour, especially if he or she claimed divine authority. I have already mentioned the inscriptions describing the judgements made by Hammurabi in Mesopotamia in the second millennium BCE: in every case he described himself as accomplishing divine wishes. More recently, the assumption of responsibility by the chief or king for seeing that the laws were observed has been documented in the Anglo-Saxon tribes. At first, minor crimes could be expiated by a payment, but later any crime was seen not only as an action against the wronged individual but also as breaking the 'King's peace', so that a double penalty was imposed[1].

From that stage, moral rules and values and secular laws have evolved in keeping with the demands of the society in question. Rulers and religious specialists introduced rules ensuring that their position and judgements should be respected. Other rules were introduced as needed. These further rules I refer to as precepts, and most are compatible with the Golden Rule of Do-as-you-would-wish-others-to-do-to-you or some variant thereof. Thus the Commandments not to steal or bear false witness and so on are acceptable because one does not want to be robbed or lied about oneself.

But our morality involves something much more subtle than merely obeying rules. This has been shown by 'thought experiments'. A railway trolley is careering down a track and five people will be killed if nothing is done. Should it be diverted down a sidetrack when that would kill one person who was standing there? Here intention seems to be fundamental. Most people see it as acceptable to allow the trolley to kill one person as an unintended by-product of saving five, but not acceptable to deliberately push someone in front of the trolley with the same effect[76, 77]: it is the intention that matters. However, allowance must be made for cultural factors: parents who believed that it was wrong for parents to hit children took a different view if the question referred to a culture in which parents believed that misbehaving children were possessed by an evil spirit which could be exorcised by spanking[160]. In each case it was seen as moral for the parent to act in a way culturally perceived as appropriate. How far lack of intention should be accepted as an excuse for anti-social behaviour is an important issue to which there seems to be no clear answer. 'It was an accident' is often taken as exonerating an individual from culpability, but should more care have been taken to prevent the accident?

There are at least two ways in which precepts arise. Some are formulated by leaders who, as we have seen, have often claimed divine guidance in their judgements. Others are a consequence of dialectical influences between what people do and what they are supposed to do. I mentioned the example of the respectability of divorce in chapter 1: as another example, in the nineteen thirties it was considered sinful for a couple to live together if they were not married. After World War Two premarital cohabitation became more usual, and as it became more frequent it became more accepted and even to be seen as a useful preliminary to marriage[45].

As yet another example, homosexual relations were not only considered immoral but were actually illegal in the nineteen fifties in Britain. As more homosexuals openly declared the nature of their sexuality, it became more usual and less disreputable, and as it became more overt, homosexuality gradually became more widely accepted. In this case the efforts of a small number of intellectuals led to homosexuality ceasing to be illegal, though some fundamentalist Christians continued to consider it sinful and it remains unacceptable to a sizeable proportion of the population.

Sunstein[144] argues that many of our moral judgements result from using heuristics that provide the right answer in the great majority of cases, but can lead to an inappropriate answer in rare cases. Thus the heuristic 'Do not knowingly cause a human death' works well for most of the time, but should it be applied to the government that allows nuclear weapons, or a new highway to be built, or tobacco to be sold, when it knows that deaths will result? No doubt opinions will differ (see also ref [168]).

The acquisition of morality by individuals
Genes and experience
Again, I shall treat this issue briefly since my only aim is to indicate that the way in which individuals assimilate the rules, values and conventions of their society is ceasing to be a mystery. Here it is important to stress that the old dichotomy between behaviour that is 'instinctive', 'innate', 'inborn' or 'genetically determined' and behaviour that is learned or acquired is now passé. All behaviour depends on both the genetic constitution of the individual and on his/her current and past experience[12], though the relative importance of these two sources of influence differs according to the behaviour in question and context. It may make sense to talk of differences between individuals, or changes over time, being due to differences in genetic factors or in experience, but not to speak of characteristics as

one or the other. Individuals may have *predispositions* to acquire some values and types of behaviour and not others[91, 132]. Thus the probable ubiquity of the Golden Rule does not imply that it is somehow encoded in human genes, but that all humans, given certain commonalities in their experiences, are prone to develop (not necessarily conscious) respect for the Golden Rule. An important part of those experiences may be the society of others who also subscribe to the principle of reciprocity. A recent account of the complexity of development has been given by Bateson & Gluckman[18] (see also ref[64]).

The role of the caregiver
A popular misconception about moral development is that the sole parental task is to eliminate the 'bad behaviour' that is inherent in all children. In fact, very young humans have propensities to please their parents, to be good, and to cooperate. The smile, developing by about one month, is a means towards establishing a good relationship with the caregiver. It is in the baby's interests to please the caregiver because that makes it more likely that the caregiver will give more care. Fourteen month old children will try to help an adult with her hands full to open a door; two year olds will try to pick up something that an adult has dropped[148]. Of course babies dirty their nappies, but that is part of their nature. They cry and make a nuisance of themselves by demanding attention, but this also is behaviour with which they are naturally endowed in order to ensure that they get the care that they need: it should not be seen as bad however irritating it is to the parent. Parents are inclined to attribute intentionality to children before it is appropriate to do so, but behaviour that can legitimately be called 'bad' cannot appear until the baby is old enough to be conscious of its intentions and turn them into actions. Children are born with propensities that we see as partly 'good' and partly 'bad', into a world that their parents see as partly 'good' as well as partly 'bad'. Ambivalence and conflict are present in both child and environment. Parents encourage what they perceive as 'good' behaviour as well as discouraging what they perceive as 'bad', though parental views of what is 'good' and what is 'bad' differ between cultures. In any case, parents may build on predispositions[91, 132] to learn this rather than that, such as the predispositions to please the parent or the selfish assertive tendency for the child to get what it wants.

We now know a great deal, though certainly not everything, about why some people grow up to be predominantly prosocial and others to be more selfishly assertive. Some differences are genetically influenced, but very early interactions and relationships with a principal caregiver, normally a parent, are of crucial importance. It is virtually certain that in all societies the development of the propensity to behave prosocially stems from the nature of the mother/child (or principal caregiver/child) relationship[24, 141]. Children with mothers who are sensitively responsive to their needs, loving, but also impose gentle but reasoned discipline, tend to be secure, confident in themselves and with others. 'Sensitively responsive' does not mean that the mother is always positive to the child, but rather that she reads the child's behaviour accurately and responds appropriately. In this way she comes to serve as a 'secure base' who is there for the child when needed. She will also provide boundaries for the child. Children who are brought up in this way tend, other things being equal, not only to be prosocial with peers but also to develop into considerate adults[24, 31]. But children with anxious mothers are likely to be less secure in their attachment to their mother[140, 141]. Indeed a synthesis of many studies, including studies in non-western cultures, has shown that maternal sensitivity is significantly associated with a secure mother-child relationship[44] (Note 8).

Certain aspects of the early environment into which children are born, and in which early development takes place, are broadly similar everywhere and have been described collectively as the 'environment of evolutionary adaptedness'[24] (see Note 9). All young humans are adapted to suck at the maternal breast, and to find security in the proximity of the mother. But the precise behaviour by which infants express their emotions about separations from and reunions with the mother may be both culture-specific and influenced by the mother/child relationship. Furthermore the cultures into which babies are born vary greatly[66], as do the precise techniques used during development to encourage the further development of prosociality – reinforcement, reasoning, modelling and so on also differ between societies[163]. For instance, most hunter/gatherers, unlike western parents, place much emphasis on sharing food[21, 81, 106] and in some societies young children are deliberately taught to share, whereas sharing is not seen as so important by many western parents; and many groups consider an individual's attitude to ancestors to be of prime importance, while in other societies preceding generations are soon forgotten.

Of course the early relationship with the mother is only a foundation: our propensities to show prosocial behaviour or selfish assertiveness are also influenced by subsequent experience. Early experience sets the stage by placing constraints on what the child is likely to experience, and predisposing him/her to seek out some kinds of experience and not others. A mother in a group experiencing food shortage who has to spend a large amount of her time and energy finding food may not have time to give her child the tender loving care that it needs: such foetal or child experiences will affect the child's personality in due course. It also affects the resilience with which the growing child copes with the vicissitudes of life. This is especially true of mothers who live in poverty in an otherwise affluent society (p. 60). Similarly, but for quite different reasons, affluent parents may deny their children the personal loving care that their children need.

Later the wider social environment becomes important, the peer group being of special importance in mediating cultural influence on individual development[33], though its influence depends on what has gone before. Some have believed that everyone succumbs to the power of the group, and that once you are in an anti-social group it is almost impossible to resist its influence. But this neglects the complexity of the experiential and social factors that dispose people to join groups. Not all groups are violent, and experimental evidence shows that individuals are less likely to join groups with tyrannical or anti-social norms the more their membership of other groups is salient and the more they are made accountable to those alternative groups[75]. In such situations, prosocial group norms need strong leadership to survive, and strong leaders are effective because they convince their followers that what they are doing is in the followers' interest, and especially when they can convince their followers that the Right is on their side and that they are threatened by evil outsiders. As we have seen too often in recent history, in many cases people do great wrongs because they believe they are right and actively identify with groups whose ideology justifies the oppression of others. They may even strive to outdo each other in their efforts to foster goals that others see as evil.

Perhaps I should emphasize that these are generalisations, selected to give an impression of the progress, and also the difficulties, in understanding the nature of child development. Even the model of the two propensities is only an heuristically useful device, and although much progress has been made, unravelling all the complexities is still a gargantuan task.

Differences in experience tend to lead to differences in how individuals see themselves – that is their self-concepts. It is useful at this point to elaborate on the idea of the 'self-concept'.

The self-concept

In interpreting people's behaviour, including one's own, it is convenient to use a concept of 'self'. Our behaviour changes with time and situation, but we explain the continuity in our lives by postulating that we each have a 'self'. This says nothing about the nature of the 'self' – it is a useful concept for saying something about how we see ourselves and others. It takes a few years for a human baby to acquire a sense of self, and it seems to be primarily, though not exclusively, a human characteristic.

There are inevitable cultural and situational influences on the nature of the self-concept. For instance, as a broad generalisation, Westerners tend to see themselves as individuals and in terms of what they do, accomplish or possess: 'I am a man, tall, Christian, good at football, reasonably well-off, living in such-and-such street'; while those from eastern, more 'Collectivist' cultures give more precedence to the groups to which they belong: 'I am a man, I belong to the local Church and I play for the local football team'. Much of the information we use in describing ourselves comes from observing how others behave towards us, or rather from how we perceive others to perceive us. In addition, how one sees oneself depends in part on recent experiences and on the situation one is in. A woman psychologist in the company of people from other disciplines will see herself as a psychologist, but in the company of male psychologists will see herself as a woman[113]. In addition, one sees oneself as a different kind of person according to the situation one is in, at work and home for instance: the situation becomes part of the self-concept as we see ourselves as 'me-at-home' or 'me-at-work'. It will be clear that the concept of 'self' is slippery, but it is nevertheless useful in the present context.

Now we store in our minds (brains) certain values and rules of conduct. These can be seen as part of the self-concept. 'I am male, married, manager of a small business, a little shy …' and also as 'honest, reliable, concerned with truth, agnostic,' and so on. This provides us with a useful way of talking about the nature of the 'conscience'. When we see ourselves behaving or intending to behave in ways that are incompatible with the values or precepts stored in our self-concept, we feel guilt or shame. In addition, if we see someone else behaving in ways that are incompatible with the values that we feel ought to be guiding their behaviour, we feel righteous indignation (as discussed on p. 32). Perhaps I should reiterate, the self-concept is a useful model, but carries no implication that it involves a specific physiological mechanism.

It has been suggested that every individual tries to maintain 'congruency' between how she sees herself (i.e. her self-concept), how she sees herself to be behaving or intending to behave, and how she sees others to perceive her. Thus a woman who sees herself as intelligent but perceives others not to share her view, experiences a lack of congruency (incidentally, a common experience amongst students who have been the best pupil at school when they arrive at university). Lack of congruency may lead to attempts to restore it. The individual may misperceive the evidence, interpret ambiguous evidence as confirming her self-concept, or be especially sensitive to evidence that is compatible with her own view of herself. She may accept praise, but disregard contrary evidence as unreliable[11]. We prefer to be with others who confirm our self-concept, and so on. All these are familiar dodges when one examines one's own behaviour. And, perhaps also though less strongly, we defend the integrity of the environments or communities we have incorporated in our self-concepts (see also ref [19]).

The media
One's self-concept, how one sees oneself, and how one sees how one should behave, is continuously influenced by, and indeed incorporates, the culture in which one lives. In the modern world the media are powerful in forming our views and we must ask how far the picture of the world that they give us is an accurate one?[93] Many journalists do what they can to provide accurate reports, but there are substantial obstacles in the way. Perhaps those who come nearest are the TV reporters in the field, on the spot of a natural disaster or enmeshed in a military unit in action, who report directly to their audience as the news happens before their eyes. But even they inevitably have personal biases, and may have conditions imposed on what they report by local (e.g. military) authorities. And as soon as their reports are filtered by their editors at base, editorial bias may

affect both what is served up to the public and its interpretation.

Most journalists do not have the luxury of being on the spot, though luxury is perhaps not the right world for those who endure hardships and danger to get the news. Most journalists sit in offices far removed from the action and use information fed to them by their computer screens, much of which comes from PR people, paid by their masters (in institution, government, political party or what have you) to purvey the news, often with a particular slant. Occasionally the PR representatives speak directly to the public, but more usually their role is not apparent and they provide a ready source of information for the journalists.

Quite apart from the biases introduced by the PR people, what appears in the media is influenced internally. The owner may insist on a particular political view, and is virtually always interested in making money. This is determined by the number of copies of the newspaper sold or the size of the radio or TV audience. Thus media content is tailored to public demand, and there seems to be something attractive in the misfortunes of others: political or other important world news takes second place to horror stories, murders, rapes and divorce (p. 112). As I write, at least three wars are going on in the Middle East, and British Forces are involved in two of them, but the morning television news was concerned entirely with local crimes.

As a result of this the public could learn not to trust the media, but the surprising thing is that many seem not to care if the media are untrustworthy. The sales of some of the tabloids are vast, and their attraction seems to lie in reports that make the world seem like a dangerous or sexy place. Sensation and exaggeration may be exploited to the full. One must conclude that people buy them because of the horrors they purvey or the intimate stories of the media-created 'celebs'. There must be a demand for that sort of 'news'. The bases for that are hard to understand. Are horror stories attractive on a 'There but for the grace of God go I' basis? Are stories about celebs popular because it allows the reader to peep into a desirable but inaccessible world? Some stories are apparently read because they take celebs down a peg: one recent story told about how some pictures of a film star revealed that she did not shave under her arms.

In summary, what we get as 'news' is often distorted by the personal biases or perceived duty of diverse interested parties in its transmission from happenings in the real world to the public. Of course one must not believe everything one reads in the newspapers or sees on the TV, though the distortions are not primarily due to deliberate lying, but rather to the complexity of the network between the actual world and what is presented for public consumption. The incumbents of each link in that network, including reporter, PR people, editor and proprietor, are constrained by the requirements of their own roles. Their livelihood may depend not on the quality or veracity of what they write, but on the extent to which it conforms to what is expected of them. Maintaining one's own true self is not always easy. Is it possible that there is a parallel between the religiosity of those who feel they profit from attending religious services but do not accept the religious myths, and those who read the tabloids knowing them to be unreliable?

Summary
This chapter is concerned:
1. With how morality arose in evolution, where the difficult problem is the origin of prosociality. Several processes are likely to have been involved. Especially important was probably competition between small groups, where groups with individuals who cooperated and behaved prosocially with other members of their own group would have been at an advantage. Members of other groups could be treated as rivals. However even within the group individuals tended to look after their own interests: morality maintained the balance between prosociality and selfish assertiveness to in-group members. Reciprocity was important in maintaining prosociality. When leaders emerged, they acquired a central role in maintaining order.
2. The early mother-child relationship is crucial in establishing basic predispositions but these may be modified by subsequent experience.
3. The self concept, how an individual sees him/herself, is useful in helping us to understand the nature of the conscience. The self-concept is affected by the context, including the often misleading picture of the world purveyed by the media.

4

Where our Current Morality Fails

Given the state of society, we might be tempted simply to abandon the moral rules that are now accepted. But our morality has played an essential part in holding our societies together. So let us try to identify where it fails in order to try to build something better. In the following discussion I shall not make a clear distinction between principles, precepts and conventions, except where ubiquity or malleability is an issue.

Independence from religious beliefs
A new morality must be independent of any religious belief system. As discussed in chapter 2, moralities have long been associated with belief systems and each may affect the other, but I have argued in chapter 3 that the early evolution of morality was probably independent of religion. Here I suggest that religious *belief* should not be used as a basis for morality: whether other aspects of religion facilitate prosocial behaviour is an open issue.

Religions have both good and bad consequences for their adherents, and most of the bad ones depend on beliefs or differences in belief. The Christian church's belief system has often been, and sometimes is at present, conducive to conflict within and between churches as well as being used to further inter-group conflict and war. Codes based on (supposedly) Christian principles led to the cruelty and inhumanity of the Crusades and the Inquisition: in World War One both sides believed the Christian God was on their side. Differences in belief have been the source of, or justification for, an enormous amount of conflict and suffering. Even, indeed perhaps especially, differences in belief between closely similar religious groups, for instance Protestant and Catholic, or Sunni and Shia, have led to violent conflict.

The pronouncements of religious leaders are seen as authoritative, and this has exacerbated conflict between religions and between sects, as well as causing personal suffering. The Roman Catholic Pope's pronouncements on reproductive behaviour have exacerbated both the spread of sexually transmitted diseases and the world's population problems. Religious beliefs have been used to support secular power, sometimes with beneficial consequences and sometimes with harmful ones. Religious beliefs in some countries foster unfairness for women and gay people. And some New Testament suggestions, such that you should reject your family if they do not agree with you (Matthew, 10, 35), are not always conducive to a happier society. So a search for a new morality must not depend on belief in the validity of dictates in the Bible or any other supposedly holy book: indeed any form of religious extremism is likely to lead to trouble. Selective quotation from either the Bible or the Koran has been the cause of much suffering and even war. At the same time, as discussed in chapter 2, we must not deny that the Biblical narratives and rituals can have value if their nature is understood, or that many claim satisfaction from participating in religious ritual.

I should add that secularism that frowns on certain religiously inspired customs, such as the wearing of a burkha, is also controversial for many. The dangers of extremism may apply there too.

Religiosity and moral behaviour.
If morality is an aspect of religion, one might expect that individuals who saw themselves as religious would behave more morally than those who made no claim to be religious. Probably all religions encourage prosociality, especially but by no means exclusively to in-group members, and many punish selfish assertiveness. It has therefore been suggested that religion is a biological adaptation that promotes group integration: whether or not that is the case, group integration is certainly a consequence of religion. As a result, as just mentioned, it may have fostered prosociality within groups but contributed to conflict between groups with different beliefs.

Of more interest is the influence of religiosity today on people's behaviour. Does being religious imply that an individual will behave more morally than one who is not? Clearly this is a tricky area of research: what does 'being religious' imply and can it be measured? Furthermore, most of the studies involve self-reports: that people who say they are religious also say that they live moral lives is only to be expected. Many are correlational: no such study can show that religion causes prosociality, that prosociality fosters religion, neither or both. Some studies reported on page 33 do report a positive influence of religiosity on prosociality in experimental situations. However the meta-analysis, putting all known reputable studies together, provides a fairly clear picture. There is strong evidence that individuals who describe themselves as religious, for instance claiming to pray and go to church, also describe themselves as prosocial. But that is a different matter from *behaving* prosocially. Most studies show that individuals describing themselves as religious do not behave more prosocially than those who do not so describe themselves[116]. For instance, in an experimental approach subjects in a hurry were caused to pass by a confederate lying on the sidewalk and obviously needing help. There was no evidence that those who claimed to be religious were more likely to help than those who did not claim religiosity[38]. However helping in this study was recorded unobtrusively. The evidence does show that individuals are more likely to behave prosocially if they know they are being observed or if the individual's reputation in his own eyes or those of others could be enhanced by prosocial behaviour. Some experimental evidence has shown that children and adults are more apt to behave honestly if they think they are being watched[17, 135]. This, of course, is compatible with the preceding discussion of exchange theory and could have nothing to do with religion: people behave prosocially if doing so makes them seem suitable persons to deal with. Thus the evidence is that the assumed association between religious belief and prosocial behaviour could make those who feel religious both believe that they are good and be good *if* they believe themselves to be observed by others, but to what extent religion leads of itself to more moral behaviour or better health[71] is far from clear.

Criteria
The distinction between 'good' and 'bad' behaviour is often difficult for both the religious and the non-religious. We can no longer automatically accept Biblical dictates – they may have fitted an iron-age culture, but not today's. In any case, it is seldom a case of black or white, and behaviour that would be condemned in normal circumstances may be condoned in others. For instance, in some cultures killing can be partially condoned if it can be described as a *crime passionel*; and in some areas of extreme poverty infanticide is accepted because the mother is seen as unable to rear the baby[129]. If a woman gave birth in the Auschwitz concentration camp, the guards killed both mother and baby: the prisoners therefore decided to kill newborn babies to save the mother's life[43]. In English law the degree of guilt, as indicated by the severity of the sentence, can be reduced by extenuating circumstances. On the positive side, if a rich person donates a large sum to charity

hoping that it will bring public acclaim and thus advantage, is that 'good' behaviour? Is his behaviour more virtuous than that of the poor man who gives only a few pence just because the former has a larger effect on society? Here is another problem: in the short term it is people's actions that determine the nature of society, but in the longer term their motivations or intentions may be more important. This is implied in the tenth Commandment, where it is coveting that is proscribed (Exodus, 20, 17) (see p. 40).

Immutability
The image of the Ten Commandments carved in stone, which Moses brought down from Mount Sinai, implies that our moral rules are immutable: this would have been attractive to moral leaders. The perception that we must try to live by the rules that have held our society together for millennia makes intuitive sense: clearly rules must be perceived as immutable, otherwise it would be easy to find reasons for not attending to them. But in fact, as we saw in discussing the dialectic relations between what people do and what they are supposed to do, they are not unchangeable. At the risk of being repetitive, here is another example of dialectical changes in moral value. At one time it was quite respectable to own slaves. Indeed owning slaves was rationalised in many ways – for instance many held that by exposing them to Christian teaching, slaves, seen as inferior beings, were lifted out of their state of ignorance. In the UK the change came from the efforts of a few individuals, notably Wilberforce and Clarkson, who were successful in swinging opinion against the slave trade (see p. 74).

We can see the beliefs and ethical aspects of a religious system coming apart as modern Catholics try to keep their key beliefs and respect for the Pope while using contraception and allowing priests to marry. From a recent Papal statement on the use of condoms it seems as though the Roman Catholic Church is having to change its teaching in response to what the public believe and do. The churches' moralities must not lag too far behind the changes in morality in secular society, or the churches fall into disrepute. This is a problem for all moral systems. Moral rules must be seen as absolute, and yet there must be sufficient flexibility to cope with changes in societal circumstances, in the nature of humanity and in widely accepted human moral values.

A moral code is pointless unless it restricts personal freedom, yet personal freedom is widely valued: a code based solely on permitting personal total freedom would lead inevitably to social disharmony and perhaps to overpopulation; but too much emphasis on social cooperation could lead to the demise of individuality. A delicate balance is necessary: moral codes can vary only between limits if societies are to be viable.

Morality and original sin
It used to be thought that humans are intrinsically evil, and that they need religion to be brought back into the fold. Although the doctrine of original sin is now largely discarded by many Christians, the idea that humans, or at least 'other people', are likely to be evil continues in part because, as we have seen, the media report muggings, murders, rapes and so on, and rarely mention any of the many kind actions that most of us encounter every day. This predilection for news about the bad requires explanation: a speculative answer is given in chapter 10.

We have seen that in fact young children have propensities to please their parents and to behave prosocially as well as to behave with selfish assertiveness. Morality helps to maintain a proper balance between the two, though this is where the model of two propensities is clearly only a first approximation. A degree of selfish assertiveness is part of human nature and is indeed necessary if those who have strong views of any sort, 'good' or 'bad', are to assert them.

Inadequacy of simple precepts
A Christian upbringing tends to inculcate a morality in terms of 'do nots', occasionally adding 'do's'. 'Do not kill'. 'Do not tell lies'. 'Do be kind to the old and to small children'. However we need a morality focusing on values. The complexity of modern life and our own nature means that virtually every decision that we make involves conflict between incompatible moral demands, and judgements in terms of simple rules or even intentions are inadequate[84]. Our morality must be based on values. This has been especially evident in the field of reproductive biology. Is abortion, involving the killing of a potential human being, justified because it saves the mother's life or enables her to realise her potential? Is artificial insemination with a donor's sperm permissible? What are the consequences for the offspring? Some find these questions difficult to answer, and many fall back on their interpretations of a holy book.

The question of abortion has proved especially difficult: feelings have been so strong that, in the USA, a doctor practising in an abortion clinic was murdered. Is this an issue about which a woman should be allowed to make up her own mind? 'No' comes the answer, the foetus is not able to articulate its claim to life. Well then, does its claim matter? Does it know it has a claim? And so the argument goes on, but the bottom line is that the anti-abortionists claim the authority of a holy book whose interpetation is not recognised by their opponents.

Rewards and punishment
Another issue is that the rewards and punishments prescribed by religions for prosocial/antisocial behaviour mostly depend on belief in an after-life and are ceasing to be effective as belief in the literal truth of the dogma is lost. Heaven and Hell may have arisen as rationalisations of beliefs in continuity after death that were already present in human nature and were fostered by priests to support their positions. However, such threats are now seen as irrelevant by non-believers and by most believers who are not fundamentalists.

Religion-based moral codes tend to imply that external rewards and punishments will always be essential: it is implied that one behaves well in the expectation of reward or to avoid punishment: 'Blessed are the meek, for they shall inherit the earth' (Matthew, 5, 5); 'Judge not and ye shall not be judged' (Luke, 6, 37). But would we all be self-seeking if we thought we could get away with it? I suggest we would not. There are too many examples of self-sacrifice in everyday life, in the caring professions, in charity workers, in war, to accept that humans are always selfishly motivated. Some will say that these are the product of ultimately selfish motivations, motivations buried deep in the unconscious ('My mother would have approved') or are the expressions of psychological motivations ultimately the result of natural selection. That does not matter: the point is that the individual acts prosocially without (or in spite of) conscious calculation of the consequences for him(her)self.

Indeed, what we now know about moral development only partially supports the view that moral behaviour always needs self-interested considerations (p. 43). We have seen that research on children's development indicates that young children have propensities to be good as well as bad, to please their parents as well as to behave with selfish assertiveness. Which predominates is a result of the child's experience: the evils we now see in society are at least partly the consequence of the social environments we have created. The nature of our society must therefore carry at least some of the blame for the behaviour of individuals. Poverty and wealth differentials are not only conducive to crime, but also create family situations that make it difficult for parents to show the combination of loving care and sensitive discipline that will produce adults who are less selfishly assertive (p. 44). But the reverse is also true: the behaviour and values of individuals are responsible for the nature of society. To break this vicious circle it is necessary to work at both ends of the dialectic (Figure 2).

In any case, rewards and punishments for prosocial/antisocial behaviour are already part of social living (p. 31-33). We already have propensities to punish other individuals if we disapprove of their behaviour and to reward those who behave well. In every society those who defy the accepted norms are ostracized, punished or rejected. Furthermore, gossip spreads the news about good or bad behaviour. Those who behave according to the societal norms are respected, receive adulation, or have statues erected in their honour. Heaven and hell are redundant.

There remains, of course, the question of what behaviour should be publicly honoured? One problem at the moment is that statues to men distinguished for their military achievements exceed in number those to philosophers, philanthropists, poets and others who care about the state of society. Surely this must be put right if we are to achieve a world-view more focussed on universal well-being.

Morality and institutions
Our social life has been facilitated by institutions that humankind has created for specific purposes. I include here the church, business corporations, the armed services and so on. Each is characterised by involving one or more positions, the incumbents of which have certain rights and duties as a consequence of their position. Many of the institutions on which societies depend require, encourage or permit behaviour that would otherwise be considered immoral. When in their institutional role, people believe they are doing right even though it is contrary to the morality stored in their self-systems or accepted in society: their self-concepts change from a family persona to an institutional one. I have discussed this issue in more detail elsewhere[86], so this is only a brief summary.

The Market-place and Competition.
It is intrinsic to the nature of the marketplace that sellers try to get the best price that they can and buyers pay as little as they can get away with. At the simplest level in which one individual is selling an object to another it is just accepted that both seller and buyer understand the game and will drive as hard a bargain as they can; the Golden Rule is inverted to I-am-going-to-get-as-much-as-I-can-out-of-you-because-I-know-you-are-trying-to-get-as-much-as-you-can-out-of-me and it is seen as fair to be conservative with the truth.

Many, perhaps most, economists have seen this competition as a good thing: competition between sellers keeps prices down for the consumer and the quality of the goods in question high. Transpose this to competition between companies, and Anti-Trust laws exist to maintain competition. However, at every level sellers are tempted to magnify the positive qualities of their goods and to minimize their defects in their efforts to increase sales: in other words they are tempted to lie. At the more complicated level of the company, the Chief Executive Officer may feel that his principal duty is to maximise the dividend of shareholders, but he is placed in the impossible position of having to satisfy a number of different stakeholders, for he also has duties to the workforce, the customers, his suppliers and others according to the nature of the business. The inversion of the Golden Rule may be seen to be 'justified' to some extent by the need to please the buyer, and the inversion is seen as proper policy for guiding business dealings in many contexts.

Each manufacturer tries to make sure that more of his products are sold than those of other manufacturers. Retailers add their efforts to the same end. One consequence of this market-place competitiveness in western societies has been excessive consumerism in all branches of society. We are persuaded to buy more than we need, we buy objects that we will never use, we have to have not just the best and the newest, but something better and more up-to-date than our neighbours. The belief that the price of an object is 'reduced' is a powerful incentive to buy it, whether or not one needs it. This is in part the result of the manufacturers and retail merchants trying to sell as many of their products as they can. They know how to take advantage of human selfish assertiveness to sell their wares, and must carry some responsibility for the greed that can lead to shoppers being trampled underfoot when the doors open for the January sales; for the inability of people to discriminate between what is necessary and what it would be nice to have; for the power of the credit system enabling customers to buy now and pay later; and for making goods that will soon need to be replaced. When people see themselves as consumers, it is to the detriment of their personal relationships and of other aspects of their lives.

Discussion about competition at the company level often neglects the fact that competition inevitably involves a loser as well as a winner. It may lead to putting a rival out of business, with resulting unemployment. Economists have maintained that competition is an essential part of the business world and is to be encouraged: as a result the businessman (or woman) can see his behaviour as guided by an ethic that justifies selfish assertiveness not only on the grounds that the same precept applies to all those involved, but also that the public is better served. It is easy to forget that 'A highly dynamic capitalist economy ... is necessarily continually creating new products, while seeking to produce established ones more profitably. This creativity in the pursuit of profit necessitates destroying the value of older products and the skills, companies and livelihoods of those involved in producing them'[146].

There is another aspect to this: the earth's resources are not unlimited. Consumerism leads to depletion of the 'rare earths' and other valuable materials and to pollution of the atmosphere and the resulting climatic changes. Frugality is imperative today. If India and China were to have the same number of cars per person as western countries, global warming might well be disastrous.

Unfortunately competition is becoming more and more dominant in society and seems to be taking charge of our lives. In sport, competitiveness is enhanced by the financial consequences of winning. General knowledge competitions on the television are accompanied by derision for the losers, and the competitions are nearly always competitions for money.

Competitiveness must play a part in the growing gap between rich and poor. So long as we had the Reagan/Thatcher view that capitalism is based on the belief that wealth will trickle down to the less well-off, the trend for that gap to widen seemed inescapable: it is easier for the haves to make more than the have-nots in both absolute and relative terms, and the gap inevitably widens. Ultimately, the differences between rich and poor stem largely from greed and good fortune on one side and from lack of opportunity and bad luck on the other. Markets are said to provide the buyer with freedom of choice, but what a person chooses is inevitably influenced by the size of his purse. And, as we shall see, inequality has many consequences on both health and prospects.

Other factors contribute to the wealth gap. Middle and upper class parents resent inheritance tax on the ground that striving to give one's children a good start is a powerful incentive, and that it is their right to do what they like with their assets. But it is clearly unfair that other children should be handicapped by the bad luck of having been born into a poor family. And it seems very difficult for the education system to make sure the situation is not perpetuated. Working class homes tend to have fewer books, to have fewer family discussions and to lack quiet space for study at home as compared with middle class homes. Working class parents may encourage children to leave school to get a job and augment the family income rather than facilitating their children's further study with a view to a more satisfying job or entry to university.

The situation is exacerbated by the media. In catering to public taste they feed it. By focusing on the rich and famous, the celebrity culture encourages the growth of materialism and can lead to a steady deterioration in society. The focus is on *things*: the value that many have placed on finding meaning in their lives, a meaning that comes from living in a just world, goes by the board.

We all want to acquire the things we need. It is part of our nature. But capitalism encourages excessive striving for material goods that we do not need. Advertising, an inevitable adjunct to competition, leads to consumerism. The competitive urge to have more is never satisfied: it leads to wanting more, and more and more yet again. We must have more and better than the next man.

Competition inevitably leads to inequality. Inequality, as it exists in most western societies, cannot be desirable. Given that Christian doctrine was first formulated and disseminated with the aim of winning converts amongst an underclass whose chances of bettering their situation by open revolt were extremely slender, it is not surprising that acceptance of the status quo was an important part of its message. 'Blessed are the meek …' But how should that translate in the modern capitalist world? Accepting the present situation without modification cannot lead to a better world.

There is extensive evidence, both within countries and across countries, and by many indices of well-being, that income inequality is associated with social disadvantage. In their important review of the need for greater equality, on which this account is based, Wilkinson and Pickett[164] demonstrate a close relation in developed countries between income inequality and increasing mental illness, drug use, obesity, teenage pregnancy, violence and infant mortality, decreasing life expectancy, educational achievement and social mobility. Some of the richer countries actually do worse overall than the poorer countries, implying that inferior material conditions are not the issue: rather it is the inequality within society that is the basic issue. Indeed we should probably go further than that: it is not so much inequality itself but the perception of inequality that is the issue. Inequality is also associated with a lack of trust of strangers, and the evidence suggests that it is income inequality that is the basic issue[164].

Wealth differentials also lead to inefficiency. The difference between the highest and the lowest incomes has been increasing rapidly in recent years: as a result of the increase in income differentials, employees feel the pay rates are unfair and this harms the organisation's effectiveness. Top earners can now expect to earn something approaching a million UK pounds a year. The basic pay of a Chief Executive Officer in one of the major firms is now over 80 times the average worker's salary[98]. The rewards obtained by the highest paid are just simply too great. Why should anyone need so much? It is not only that it is so easy for those involved to fail to recognise when enough is enough, but that those who gain most are not those who have contributed most.

Life expectancy increases with economic development (Gross national income per head) amongst the poorer countries, but not amongst the richer ones. Amongst the latter it is the differences between rich and poor that are crucial. With increasing income inequality, health and social problems increase. The crucial issue seems to be the differences in status that are associated with the income differences. Strong evidence shows that there has been an increase in anxiety and depression in the USA since the nineteen fifties. This, surprisingly, was associated with an apparent increase in self-esteem. However, this overall picture of increasing self-esteem has been due to two quite different effects: in one group the increase in self-esteem was associated with happiness, confidence, an ability to make friends and so on, but there was also a second group who scored high on self-esteem but tended to racism, violence and insensitivity in personal relationships. In this second group the self-esteem involved a denial of weakness and an attempt to maintain a positive sense of self in the face of imagined criticism. It seems that the increase in anxiety is a consequence of increasing social stress and an inability of individuals to feel at ease with each other.

Interviewing high earning lawyers and bankers, Toynbee and Walker[150] found that those with the higher incomes were extraordinarily ignorant about what other people earn, tending to overestimate the incomes of their poorer contemporaries, as though diminishing the unfairness of their own position and trying to emphasize their own ordinariness. Toynbee and Walker comment (p. 36) 'Here are people (the higher earners) who may be technically adept, or good at deal-making, but as a group with one or two exceptions – they were less intelligent, less intellectually inquisitive, less knowledgeable and, despite their good schools, less broadly educated than high flyers in other professions ... Their high salaries were not a sign of any obvious superiority'. In our increasingly undemocratic society the income differential is self-perpetuating: rich parents mean better schooling, a better start in adult life and subsequent earning power, while poverty leads to poorer qualifications, worse jobs and poorer health. Furthermore, in Britain the situation is exacerbated by the complex devices that the rich use to avoid paying all the taxes that are due.

The bottom line is that the competitiveness encouraged by the market place leads to self-assertiveness that almost requires dishonesty, inequality in wealth, excessive consumerism, waste and inefficiency.

War and Violence
The most obvious case is capital punishment, often justified in terms of reciprocity: the executioner's duty is to kill a fellow citizen. This is especially horrifying when a citizen whose relative has been murdered is encouraged or forced to play a part in the execution of the murderer, as is the case in some countries where the principle of revenge is taken literally and blasphemy is equated with murder (see p. 36). Fortunately capital punishment has been abolished in nearly all western countries, some US States being notable exceptions.

In war, killing a member of the enemy's forces is not only condoned but also praised: in this case the victim is seen as a member of another group. The group differences are usually exaggerated by propaganda: in the two World Wars each side described the other side as evil and even sub-human. The 'Just War' doctrine, ascribed to St.

Augustin and to St. Thomas Aquinas, limits the right to make war to certain causes that are considered 'Just', but that in itself allows that killing can be justified in certain circumstances. For centuries the right to go to war was considered as virtually unlimited, but attempts to restrict aggressors were made in the Hague Peace Conferences before World War One and after it by the League of Nations and the Kellogg-Briand Pact. After the Second World War the Charter of the United Nations outlawed resort to aggression unless authorised by the Security Council. However wars, including some initiated by the United Kingdom and the United States of America, have continued to break out in many parts of the world.

There are, however, officially sanctioned restraints on killing even in wartime. Dum-dum (i.e expanding) bullets were outlawed internationally in 1868, and poison gas after the First World War, though both of these conventions have been broken since. The behaviour of those in command at each level is governed by 'rules of engagement' determining how far they should go in pursuing 'military necessity'. Unfortunately it is often extremely difficult to abide by such rules in the heat of combat. The deaths of civilians are written off as collateral damage, a necessary consequence of all-out war. Furthermore the duty imposed on combatants by commanders may conflict with the demands of morality. In World War Two many bomber crews were placed in exactly that dilemma: Johnson[102] has given a tragic account of how, as a bomber pilot, he was caught between his duty and the knowledge that the devastation and suffering that he was causing was morally wrong. The courageous lone voice of Bishop Bell in the House of Lords, condemning the bombing of civilians, was disregarded on the grounds of the necessity of winning the war. (I feel it is necessary to emphasize that this is not intended to belittle the extraordinary bravery of those who served in Bomber Command, nor their colleagues in the US Air Force. Nor, regrettably, does it imply that war is never necessary). The failure of the Coalition in the Iraq War to publish or even give estimates of the number of military or civilian casualties on the other side is another example of the morally unbalanced thinking that is an inevitable consequence of war.

The morality of weapons of mass destruction pose problems of another degree of magnitude. The incredible suffering caused by the nuclear weapons dropped on Hiroshima and Nagasaki at the end of World War Two is impossible to describe or even imagine. At the time it was misleadingly justified as saving the American lives that would have been lost in a seaborne invasion of Japan, but even that involves the presumption that Japanese lives are less important than American lives – a type of assumption inherent in any war but difficult to justify on moral grounds. In peacetime leaders have supported the retention of nuclear weapons even though they are unable to specify any situation in which they might be used and when they know that they could never personally authorise their use. Vast sums are spent on nuclear weapons when the money is urgently needed for social purposes. The Cold War saw an enormous build-up of nuclear weapons that it is proving very difficult to reverse.

Torture techniques are another by-product of the institution of war. After the assault on the Twin Towers terrorism became portrayed as an imminent threat in the West. Suspect individuals were incarcerated and tortured because it was believed that they knew the plans, but would not talk. Torture techniques, previously constrained by the Geneva Convention, were extended by politicians in 2002 to include water-boarding (and other techniques), and the American President decided to abandon the Geneva Convention. There was an inevitable backlash, and the constraints of the Geneva Convention were restored[127].

Democracy
We have a democratic government, and democracy is probably the best form of government one can have. But we have not yet come to terms with the problems that it raises. To get elected to the British Parliament you have to convince the voters that you will promote the policies that they think they need. But the voters do not all think alike, even if one considers only those who will vote for the same party, and the candidate may be tempted to bias what he says to suit his/her perception of the electorate. Once elected the candidate may be forced by the Whip to toe the party line and vote in a way not in accordance with his conscience, so he or she is in effect lying. If he does not support the party line he (or she) will lose chances of preferment in the party. The whole Party may find it tactically desirable to vote at variance from its pre-election pledges. The Party leader may be forced to distort the truth in order to get the support he desires. I am deliberately not mentioning specific cases because this is not the place for Party-political discussion, but all the above problems have affected British politics in the last 15 years[86]. None of

this is saying that Democracy is not the best political system for us but, as Runciman[126] has convincingly shown, hypocrisy is inevitable.

In addition, given the aftermath of wars in the Middle East and in Africa, we must recognise that some countries are simply not ready for democracy. Corruption and lack of an adequate legal system and police force can make an attempt to establish democracy impossible[90].

Similar problems appear over world governance. Delegates must choose between what is best for their own country and what is best for the world, and are subjected to almost irresistible pressure towards the former. The secure seats on the Security Council, assigned to the victors in the aftermath of World War Two, are no longer appropriate. The ability of a few countries to veto decisions of a majority is the opposite to democratic. But since any attempt to change the system in the direction of democratic world government, or at least to a system fair to all, must be immune to the veto, it is hard to see how change can occur. Perhaps the forces of globalisation will prove irresistible.

Religion
Religion requires that even officials of the Church may feel themselves forced to be economical with the truth. Missionaries may expound the book seen as holy in their church as if it were literally true even when they know it is a myth, even though they see it as a myth with important moral implications. Worse still, officials of the Church may lie to cover up the inappropriate behaviour of church members because they see it as their duty to protect the reputation of the church. A number of examples have recently come to light as the Roman Catholic Church attempted to cover up paedophilia amongst its priests. At a more trivial level, the Church sometimes has to find ways to circumvent its own rules. For instance, the Church of England does not recognise marriages performed in university college chapels, but a dispensation to allow them can be obtained from the Archbishop of Canterbury.

A special problem arises when the church is established as part of the State. This almost inevitably results in insincerity. If the church preaches equality, how far should it go in supporting the hierarchical structure of the state? If the Church preaches Peace, how can it support the wars in which the state is involved? When Britain was inflicting uncountable casualties on German civilians in World War Two, only Bishop Bell spoke out.

In general, excuses for 'bending the rules' are of three types. First, the rules themselves may be distorted, an extreme example being the inversion of the Golden Rule in simple business transactions. Second, the boundary of the in-group is seen as rigid, with different rules applied on the two sides. Thus, in war killing is proscribed within the boundary, prescribed beyond it. The nature of the out-group may be distorted by propaganda. Third, conflict between 'oughts' almost inevitably leads to the neglect of one side or a bending of the rules. The institutions that society has created distort the morality of individuals. Although moral precepts must *be seen as* absolutes, society condones and often requires exceptions.

Summary

In previous chapters, there are at least seven major reasons why religious beliefs may be misleading as reasons for regarding a moral code associated with it as absolute.

1. Religious dogma is not to be taken literally, so cannot be taken as a valid basis for a moral code.
2. There is no clear evidence that religiosity enhances prosociality.
3. There is substantial evidence for ways in which moral codes could have arisen through the operation of known mechanisms of evolutionary selection and known psychological processes.
4. Given the ambivalence inherent in human nature and the complexity of modern societies, moral conflict is inevitable and sometimes insoluble. Rules about behaviour are likely to prove inadequate.
5. Christian morality relies on outdated concepts, like Heaven and Hell.
6. Moral precepts must be seen as absolute but have some flexibility.
7. The institutions of modern societies demand that the incumbents of positions in them should abide by moral guidelines that differ from those in the everyday world.

5

Adjustments to Morality Are Possible

In previous chapters I have argued that at present we have only an unsatisfactory basis for our moral code, with the implication that we must seek for a new one. That does not mean that we should ditch the morality to which we have subscribed for centuries, but rather that we should assess its foundations and its applicability to the modern world. Many will argue that change is not possible – many Christians because of its supposed divine origin, others because change is either undesirable or impracticable. I have already argued that the origin of our morality can be understood in terms of known processes in biology, psychology and the social sciences, and that this provides a more secure basis for understanding its nature. In this chapter I argue that bringing about adjustments to our understanding of morality is not just a pipe dream.

Cultural differences in social behaviour

While cultural differences in social behaviour are obvious enough, it is only recently that they have been systematically documented. An important edited volume[34] provides numerous examples of cultural differences in the socio-cultural behaviour of children of great relevance to societal differences in prosocial and selfishly assertive behaviour. To take some examples in harmony with the present thesis, children's cooperative behaviour declines with increasing urbanization[68] and children living in extended families in which they are required to assume family responsibilities tend to show more prosocial and cooperative behaviour than those in economically complex, class-structured societies[54]. Children in east Asian and some south-American countries are more cooperative in their social interactions than North American children[61]. Such differences are influenced by cultural beliefs and norms[33, 34, 140]. That immigrants can adjust to new cultures, if not immediately at least in a generation or two, shows that possibilities for change exist in every society. Finally, even within some industrial societies, like those of the Scandinavian societies, the differences between rich and poor are much smaller than those in the UK or USA: this in itself means that some change is not impossible.

Egalitarian societies
We have seen that many of the ills in our societies are related to the marked differences in wealth and power between those at the top and those at the bottom of our hierarchical worlds. It is improbable, and perhaps undesirable, that such differences could be eliminated, but it is clearly desirable that they should be drastically reduced. Is that possible?

Strong evidence comes from studies of nomadic hunter/gatherer societies. The common ancestor of humans and the great apes probably lived in groups dominated by a single male. However Boehm[21], on the basis of extensive field-work and a survey of the anthropological literature, has shown that at least the great majority of surviving hunter/gatherer groups live in groups with several adult males, amongst whom relationships are egalitarian. This does not mean that life in such groups is all sweetness and light, nor that the individuals in these groups lack self assertiveness, but rather that any individual who is seen to be becoming too big for his boots is taken down a peg by other group members. A selfishly assertive propensity to dominate is still present, but any individual who allows it to become overt is suppressed. Even displays of anger may be frowned upon, and if one individual belittles, bullies or otherwise attempts to control another, others support the victim. This ethos of support for any individual being put upon by another implies an egalitarian ideal. It can perhaps be seen as resulting from a fear that the bully, if not restrained, may infringe the autonomy of others including any who support the victim, and implies that the supporters can rely on an egalitarian group. We can readily empathise with such behaviour: one feels irritated (to say the least) with colleagues who talk too much or try to lead a group when it is not appropriate for them to do so. Such behaviour is entirely in keeping with the moralistic aggression directed against those who behave too assertively, as found in western societies, and also with the view that what mattered in the evolution of prosocial behaviour to other group members is that *other people* should behave prosocially (see p. 32).

The processes used to suppress overly self-assertive individuals in hunter/gatherer groups may originate from gossip spreading the view that the offender is being too self-important[50, 51]. The signs of social disapproval may be quite subtle, but the offenders are sensitive to them. If subtle signs are inadequate, they may lead to the offender receiving cool treatment from others, a refusal to follow his suggestions, ridicule, and social isolation. In rare cases it may lead to the execution of the offender: in such cases, apparently to avoid the dangers of escalation, it is often arranged that the executioner should be a relative. But such extreme cases are rare, apparently because the desirability of a social ethos of egalitarianism is generally recognised. Individuals take care not to be seen as self-important: for instance the successful hunter will down-play the value of the animal he has killed and display exaggerated modesty about his achievement. What is important is that each group member should respect the individual autonomy of others. The basic issue is not the absence of a leader, but the ethos of the essential equality of all, and the willingness to act assertively to maintain that ethos. Individuals must be careful when moving from a family head role, where dominance is permitted and even required, to a band-member role, where the egalitarian ethos must be respected. Tension is not entirely absent, but is apparently preferred from that arising from inequalities.

Although within a household dominance of one individual by another is usual, these groups are characterised not only by an overall egalitarian ethos among the (mostly male) heads of families but also by an ethic of sharing between households. This involves primarily the sharing of meat after a large animal has been killed: a successful hunter may enjoy extra respect and other rewards for his success[103] but is expected to share at least some of the meat with others and be very reticent about his achievement. Since a high proportion of attempts to kill large animals are unsuccessful, and luck as well as differences in skill plays a certain role in this, sharing meat helps to ensure that everyone gets an adequate supply. Small food items are usually not shared.

The suppression of overtly assertive behaviour extends also to decision-making in the group: while it is recognized that some individuals have special skills, this is not seen as permitting them to dominate others or to have a special status in the group. Such an individual may be allowed to lead in an appropriate context, but he will be watched closely for signs of bossiness. Important decisions are made by consensus amongst the household heads. Leaders with special expertise are allowed to be only 'first among equals'. Usually they are required to be generous and to have other positive qualities, and they must behave with care in case they are seen to be breaching the ethos of equality.

The egalitarian norm, if that is an appropriate way to describe it, is by no means limited to hunter-gatherers, but is found also in some tribal societies. In many of these decisions are made by consensus, strong leadership is lacking and there appears to be an egalitarian ideology. So the evidence suggests that, on an evolutionary time-scale, an egalitarian ethos followed an authoritative one and was itself later succeeded by one involving hierarchy[57]. We do not know precisely how the ethic of not pushing yourself forward, of punishing those who do, and of sharing hard-to-obtain resources was lost in the transition from hunter/gatherer societies to the individualism of the modern western world. In most cases it was clearly related to the disappearance of face-to-face subsistence communities that were mostly static and where families (rather than individuals) owned small patches of land with nearly all production for consumption. With the advent of money and more-or-less distant markets, family relationships and a sense of the local community decreased. Differences in the importance of different types of wealth and their transmission across generations were also important[25]. The change probably took place earlier in Britain than on the continent[111].

We can speculate that as more skills were acquired in the society, nobody could be good at everything, and individuals learned that they could profit from the skills of others. Speculating again, those who claimed to be in touch with the gods could claim a special advantage. Either the religious leaders became political leaders or political leaders gained the support of religious leaders. It would have been necessary for would-be leaders to have something – resources, protection, etc. – to exchange for the sacrifice of some of the autonomy of those they led.

Some will say that that is all very well, but it does not mean that egalitarianism could flourish in the complexity of modern societies. Certainly it would require major changes in people's values that would depend on the wealth and social structure of the society. But the persistence of these egalitarian societies into the modern world provides an opportunity for us to see just how they worked, and it is important to note that the propensities that sustain them are still present in our own, though much undervalued. Most people enjoy group life, and abhor excessive self importance in others. Most people value their own autonomy but recognize that this requires respect for that of others. This requires a norm of equality: although we find it difficult to define what we mean by equality and how to achieve it, we still want to put down those members of our own group who think too much of themselves. So the psychological propensities necessary for a more egalitarian society are present in virtually everyone. The values held in the egalitarian societies just discussed are very different from the values held in the modern industrialized world, where selfish assertiveness is encouraged and often seems to predominate.

Behavioural propensities conducive to a fairer society
At the risk of repetition, it is appropriate to stress that the values and propensities important in these egalitarian societies are also present in ourselves. In the first place, we live in groups, and we possess the complex cognitive abilities necessary for handling the several relationships that each of us is engaged in. Second, familiarity breeds trust of other group members. Third, we all have a propensity to want to control others[13]. Fourth, at the same time we do not like to be bossed by others. We have a propensity to take down anyone who threatens the autonomy of others. Fifth, although individuals do not like to admit it, we all value the good opinions of others. Sixth, we are adept at forming alliances with others to achieve our aims. Seventh, we would like to live in a society in which relationships could have much less tension than is often the case today, a society in which we maintained our own autonomy and were not bossed by others. Eighth, although we like our own autonomy, we are willing to share.

Prosocial propensities in childhood
Chapter 3 cited evidence that prosociality in children in Western societies (and probably all other countries) is enhanced if the caregiver is sensitively responsive to the child's needs and uses gentle and reasoned discipline. The child's social relationships in later years can also have profound effects: growing up in a highly competitive or militaristic environment is likely to swing the balance between selfish assertiveness and prosociality in favour of the former. Less dramatic changes in both directions consequential on the dialectical relations between what people do and what they are supposed to do were mentioned in chapters 1 and 3.

Of special interest here are anthropological data showing variation in the background to the child rearing practices that lead to prosociality towards other group members[66]. Goody distinguishes two modes. In the anxious mode the world is seen as potentially dangerous and children learn to be shy and fearful, whereas in the secure mode there is a high level of mother/child intersubjectivity and interdependence with peers. For example, the fearful Semai, who are constantly raided by their Malay neighbours, see the forest is dangerous, fearing unrelated Semai and the strangers who are believed to lurk near the forest paths ready to decapitate them. The children are taught to share food and to avoid violence. They are given an image of themselves as helpless in a malevolent world. Within the band 'goodness' is defined as sharing and helping and 'badness' as anger and fighting.

In fierce societies the atmosphere is quite different: Goody gives two very different examples. The Yanomami of the Amazon rainforest constantly fear attack by rival groups and avert them by cultivating a reputation for fierceness or by pre-emptive attacks. But meat is shared and the sharing of meat is strictly formalized: a hunter is prohibited from eating meat that he has killed. Garden produce is not shared. There is no norm of older children yielding food to their younger siblings. Children are not physically punished but are strongly encouraged to retaliate if injured. However other fierce societies are quite different. The Illongot headhunters of the Phillipines stress sharing of all food within the household and sharing of game between households. Companionship between youths and between girls is encouraged, but fierceness and retaliation are not emphasized. Unfortunately I am unaware of any detailed studies of child-rearing in these societies.

Of course, most of these studies concern quite small-scale societies, and it certainly cannot be assumed that their implications can be transferred directly to complex modern societies. The background in the societies reviewed by Goody is quite different from that in most western families, and it is unfortunate that there is inadequate evidence on the children's early relationships. Data from the Buganda of Uganda suggest that sensitive responsiveness and reasoned discipline are equally important there[2].

Changes in values in adulthood
However important childhood influences on personality are, individuals can change. St. Paul's conversion on the road to Damascus may or may not be a myth, but more recent cases have been documented. For example, Colby and Damon cite the case of a girl brought up in Alabama with strong racial prejudices[37]. Forced against her will in college to sit at a table with a black girl, she came to like and respect the black girl and eventually dedicated most of her life to working for civil rights.

Amongst primarily Lutheran families in Sweden data show that a poor relationship with the parent is associated with a likelihood for a religious conversion to be sudden[67].

Changes in values in modern society
Although we feel that the moral precepts that guide our behaviour are immutable, some change is occurring all the time. I have already referred to the changes in the acceptability of divorce. Comparable dialectical processes have led to changes in many of the values surrounding sexual behaviour. Thus before World War Two in my university, if a male student were found to have a woman in his room after a certain hour, he was almost inevitably expelled. Now premarital cohabitation is not only allowed but in some circles encouraged[45].

Three cases of changes in morality in relatively recent times have been carefully analysed by Appiah[5]: duelling and the slave trade, which disappeared in the mid-nineteenth century, and foot binding amongst the élite in China which endured until the turn of the 19th/20th century. In each case the moral issues were known, though perhaps not properly digested, beforehand, but the demise of the practice occurred only when there was a change in values. Appiah describes this as a change in honour. Honour, in Appiah's view is a matter of the respect one receives, or can expect to receive, from others in one's own social category. Honour can be distinct from morality: for instance challenging another gentleman to a duel could be seen as the honourable thing to do and at the same time as morally wrong.

Duelling was illegal in the UK but the authorities turned a blind eye on it so long as it involved only members of the upper classes. Amongst the latter it was a matter of honour to issue a challenge if you were insulted by another 'gentleman', and a matter of honour to respond if you received one. When dueling was taken up by members of the middle classes, business men and such like, it ceased to be an 'honourable' gentleman's prerogative, and came to be seen as ridiculous. In this change, newspaper comments and cartoons played an important role.

Foot-binding amongst the Chinese élite involved the deformation of the feet of girls and women by tight binding over a long period. It was extremely painful for the woman, but was tolerated because a woman's bound foot was seen as exquisitely beautiful. The practice was limited to the élite, and may have owed its popularity to the fact that a woman with bound feet could walk only with difficulty and would therefore find it difficult to stray. The end of foot-binding was largely a consequence of the increasing influence of foreigners. European merchants arrived in the ports, and missionaries penetrated inland, bringing not only Christianity but, more importantly, modernity. The natural feet of the foreign women brought into relief the absurdity of the distorted feet of those whose feet had been bound. The Chinese élite came to see that the practice was seen as ridiculous by the foreigners and brought the country into disrepute. National reputation was as important as women's welfare in bringing about the change.

Slavery in the British Empire had been in the country's economic interests and the ending of the slave trade and of slavery in the British Empire may have been facilitated somewhat by a decrease in the profitability of West Indian sugar. However, the change occurred in spite of its abiding economic value to the country: conflicting views of the factors involved in the suppression of slavery have been discussed by Drescher[48]. Appiah's interesting analysis puts the emphasis on the role of reformers, Quakers and others, in convincing the country that a practice that was so immoral should not be allowed. This led to petitions to Parliament with hundreds of thousands of signatures. The working classes came to identify with the slaves and the position of servility and unremitting labour that they had to endure. In this case the standards of honour and morality were identical: slave owners lost honour in the sight of their peers.

The common factor in these three cases is that a practice previously seen as acceptable and honourable in the relevant section of society came to be seen as wrong. With duelling and foot-binding the change occurred in the section of society in which the practice was endemic, though the change was influenced by the opinions of a wider public. With the slave trade it was a much wider public that helped to bring about the change. How far this can be generalized to other changes in morality is open to question: changes in the law about homosexuality in Britain were due to relatively few members of the intellectual élite, and initially it remained unacceptable to the majority of the population.

In each case the change can be seen as exemplifying the dialectic between what people do and what they are supposed to do as suggested in chapter 1. And in each case the change in opinion can be seen as a change in the self-concepts of those involved under the influence of outside opinion, as mentioned in chapter 3. The important point for the present discussion is that they show that change can be made to happen.

Summary
Several considerations indicate that change is possible. Cultural differences exist, and egalitarian norms are present in some (small scale) societies. They are based not on, or not so much on, increased prosociality, but a tendency to put down those who behave overtly self-assertively. Similar behavioural propensities are present in individuals in western societies. They can be enhanced by caregivers in early development and by the peer group.

Prosocial propensities are present in children, and changes in moral values can occur both in individuals and in societies.

6

Limitations on Change

In Chapter 5 I argued that a change in our morality is possible. We already have the psychological propensities that could lead to a more equitable society. But it is vital to understand that the necessary changes in our outlook will not be achieved easily. It may not happen in our lifetimes, nor in our children's lifetimes, and perhaps not in our grandchildren's. But it will never happen if we do not start to work for it now. In doing so, we must accept that some limitations are inevitable. This chapter brings together some reasons for caution, some of which have been implicit in what has been said already.

Do not hope for a Utopia
It is undeniable that our society is not as most of us would like it to be. At least part of the problem boils down to old-fashioned greed. In terms of the model I have used for heuristic purposes, such curbs on selfish assertiveness that our society possesses are very weak: prosociality and care for the community take a back seat. There was a time within my lifetime (and this is not just harking back to the Good Old Days) when you could be pretty hopeful that if you dropped your wallet, someone would hand it in to the police station; or if a shopkeeper gave too much change, the customer would return it. In Cambridge the Sunday papers were left in a pile on the pavement with a cap beside them: it was assumed that if you took a paper you would put the money in the cap. Not so today. I do not want to make a generalisation here about changes in morality over time: in some ways society may be more moral and in some ways less moral, and much depends on the time span over which the comparison is made. But greed is everywhere in our society, and greed is both a result and a cause of the excessive materialism that surrounds us. Those who have want more, and much of our society is directed to creating new things for us to want. There seems to be no limit to the things some people feel they must have: a second home in the Caribbean, a yacht, a private jet? And in part because the more you have, the easier it is to get more, the gap between rich and poor increases.

With cultural norms as they are, none of us is immune to their influence, and that includes me. It is too easy to be blind to the suffering of those whom the present system drives into poverty. And,

Limitations on Change

as I wrote in Chapter 1, it is difficult for those who live in a first world country to even imagine the lot of many in sub-Saharan Africa, or in the slums of Mumbai or São Paulo. Just try to think what it must be like to live in a community where infanticide is accepted because half-starved mothers are unlikely to be able to rear a child. Or where food and clean water are difficult to obtain, and there can be no hope that things will ever be better. But it need not be so.

We have seen (Chapter 5) that egalitarian societies have been possible where a more egalitarian society was the accepted goal. Change is possible, but not overnight. We do not yet know enough to deal with all the problems, but we must not let idealism sink in the sea of reality. Many, perhaps most, problems involve conflicting issues. While we need moral rules, values or goals may be more important: faced with a new problem, rigid rules may not provide reliable guidance, but values and goals (ideals) are more likely to lead us to an optimal decision.

Just because new problems are constantly arising, and just because moral conflict pervades so many of the decisions we must take, it would be virtually impossible to produce a set of guidelines for solving every dilemma and it is the general principles underlying morality that we must focus on first. The judgements we make now are rooted in the existing code, which is rooted in turn in our nature. Reciprocal exchange, and some variant of the Golden Rule of 'do-as-you-would-be-done-by' are probably basic to all cultures. Ultimately, we deplore the use of nuclear weapons because we would not want them used on us, or because we identify with those on whom they would be used, or because it would be detrimental to what we see as the 'common good'. We deplore environmental pollution in part for similar reasons: it may affect us or our descendants, and the polluters are receiving benefits that far outstrip their own costs, while imposing costs on others. We are unhappy about the excessive incomes of some people in the commercial and financial sections not just because we are envious but because of the effects of wealth differentials on so many aspects of society (p. 60). I am suggesting, as many have done before, that the way forward is a greater emphasis on the community and less on self advancement.

The goal must be limited
One must accept that a perfect and universally acceptable moral code is beyond our reach. Cultures are so different, people are so different,

times change, new problems are constantly arising. We have seen that individuals and institutions are adept at finding let-outs to almost any rule. And more specifically:

1. Some conflict between individual autonomy and the social order is inevitable. As we have seen, morality holds a balance between prosociality and selfish assertiveness. Individuals tend to assert their own interests, but a world in which individualism was allowed full rein would be socially impossible. On the other hand, there will always be cheats, and if the balance favoured prosociality to any considerable degree, society could be taken over by free-riders. The law can be seen in part as an attempt to underwrite rationally the precepts and prohibitions of the moral code, ensuring a balance between prosociality and selfish assertiveness by punishing excesses of the latter.

2. Nearly every morally significant decision we make involves conflict between incompatible considerations. It may be just an internal matter: do I have time to stop and help the needy traveller lying by the road? It may be pragmatic: does a child with an incurable disease have as much right to a limited resource as a healthy child with the prospect of a constructive life ahead of her? Perhaps values conflict: it is wrong to kill, but could I help to stop a greater evil by joining the army? Individuals' duties may conflict with societal morality: perhaps one feels that one has a duty to one's employer that conflicts with spending time with one's family. A list of possible conflicts would be almost endless[84]. Simple rules will not provide adequate guidance, and we must accept that life is full of contradictions, and there is seldom a simple choice between right and wrong.

3. Morality, and indeed the law, will not necessarily be the best for all the people in a society: it may be engineered by one sub-group in order to bind others to its will, or it may be a botched-up code compromising what is believed to be best for several different sub-groups. Tension and change are both inevitable and proper.

4. Almost by definition, a successful moral code must be conducive to social cohesion, and so can vary only within limits: nevertheless there can be no absolute moral code, valid for all people at all places in all times. A morality promoting social well-being in one society might not fit in another living in a different environment and with a different history.

5. Related to the preceding points, many of the problems that

societies face will be new problems, arising from scientific advances and cultural changes. Old rules cannot always be trusted. In the modern world, giving preference to one's kin, leaving many descendants, or pushing the interests of one's kin group, are no longer seen as proper or as natural as they used to be. However, moral codes must be derived from shared views about how others should behave in the interests of social harmony, so a morality must be based in human propensities that are conducive to that end (with no implication that all that is natural is good).
6. Current codes are likely to have been based on aspirations that served well in the past, and may serve as a starting point for the future. But the present is not like the past, and the precise shape of the future is not predictable. Our morality must adjust. Institutions respected by many, like the Christian Church, are unlikely to embrace change readily. And one must always ask whether one is biased in one's certainty that one is right and the rest of society is wrong.

Is morality *passé*?

Many may say there is no value in fiddling with morality, that is old-fashioned stuff and nobody bothers with it now. That of course is the point, it is just because people disregard morality that we are in this situation. Such people may go on to say that the problems lie in our political and economic systems: if we had a different political or financial system people would behave more responsibly, or there would be less crime, or fewer teenage pregnancies. But, as I argued in the first chapter, causation is not solely one-way. It is central to the thesis of this book that how individuals behave, what they value, their culture and political and economic systems, are interconnected, each affecting the others. This was illustrated in Figures 1 and 2: how people behave is affected by the political and business/commercial systems, and also affects the nature of those systems. There is always plenty of discussion about our political and economic systems, but too little about our values and morality. The values we respect should be crucial in shaping our financial and political systems. We must attempt to redress the balance, starting from the bottom level, of how people behave and the values they hold. If they are changed in a manner that is conducive to the general good, perhaps political and economic systems that also are conducive to the same end will be easier to find.

Cultural differences
What is right in the western world is not necessarily the same as what is right everywhere in the world. Generalising broadly, those who grew up in communist China and mid-West United States have very different ways of behaving and attitudes to life. The behaviour that is seen as correct, the things that people value, depend in part on the nature of the society and the culture in which they live. As I have suggested, certain principles, in particular the Golden Rule and reciprocity, are probably essential if group living is to be possible, but moral precepts and values may differ to some extent between societies. And within a culture the moral values and rules tend to form a consistent whole. It is a mistake to think that a society, recently exposed to western culture, can immediately adopt all western values, including democracy.

Is the time ripe?
I have argued in chapter 2 that, in spite of religion's many problems, the time may not be ripe simply to discourage religion: its stories may not be true but they provide comfort to many and there may be no need to take that away precipitously. Beliefs too firmly held can do much harm, but the stories contain lessons of importance for modern society.

One might ask the same about morality. Is our society ready for a change in our values? We must learn from the floundering attempts to impose western type democracy on Iraq and Afghanistan: democracy can flourish only if certain types of societal structures, of behaviour and of values, are there already. You cannot impose a particular brand of morality on any society any time anywhere. But that is not what I am proposing. What we need is, first, an understanding of the nature of morality. As we understand more, we shall see what adjustments are needed in our culture and how they are to be made. Some suggestions are made in the remaining chapters.

In this chapter I have suggested that, although the need for change in our morality and indeed in our world-view is great, we must not expect that change will come easily.

7

Morality: Four Basic Issues

The remaining chapters provide the conclusions to which the previous chapters have led. The aim must be not to abandon the system of morality that we have at present, but to see how it can be adjusted for the modern world. Our morality must be self-supporting, dependent on issues that are already part of human nature to constrain what individuals do. It must also be seen as absolute, but with some flexibility to mesh with the problems that are appearing with changes in our societies.

But first a few words to recapitulate and slightly extend the basic concepts used in the previous chapters, summarizing them and the approach used. The selfishness, greed and materialism that plague our society are often ascribed to our financial and political systems: the route to a more satisfactory society is generally seen to require a change in the way society is organised through such systems. But causation acts both ways: the 'bottom' level of how we behave and what we value is not only influenced by, but also influences the financial and political systems we have created. This book takes a 'bottom up' approach and attempts to understand the nature of our moral systems and how they can be changed to increase well-being. Thus it is not concerned directly with political and economic systems but with the moral guidelines that pervade, to a greater or lesser degree, all levels from the man in the street to the boardroom and Cabinet office. Improvements in society depend on changes in and adherence to morality as much as, and perhaps as a necessary preliminary to, changes to political and financial systems.

Moral rules and values are necessary because of the need to preserve a balance between the propensities of individuals to look after their own interests (or what they perceive to be their interests) and their propensities to be prosocial. Balance between these two propensities is essential if a group is to be stable and harmonious. The role of morality is to preserve that balance.

This, of course, is only a framework that helps to reconcile a number of facts about what we know about human behaviour. I have stressed repeatedly that the distinction between the propensities for selfish assertiveness and prosociality is of heuristic value at a certain level of analysis, but it sometimes fails when applied to particular aspects of behaviour. For instance, to behave prosocially in a society of predominantly selfishly assertive individuals requires a degree of assertiveness. The concept of a balance between propensities in individuals provides a framework that is useful as an heuristic device, but only up to a point.

At one level morality is often seen as a set of rules, in the form of do's and don'ts, about how one 'should' or 'should not' behave. I have argued that 'values' or 'goals' may be more useful. If we seek for a generalisation as to why the rules are as they are, most of the do's and don'ts refer to behaviour that affects, one way or the other, the harmonious nature of our society.

In previous publications I have suggested that it is useful to make an (admittedly fuzzy) distinction between moral Principles and moral Precepts. Principles are almost certainly universal in all cultures, and may be seen as essential for the continuing viability of any human group: precepts, as we have seen, may have only limited generality. For example, parental care is universal in mammals; and people in nearly all cultures express disapproval verging on horror when parents do not care for their children: our cultural concept that child care is a duty for parents is a reification of the results of natural selection (see p. 31). Concepts of exchange, fairness and the Golden Rule are probably also ubiquitous, though they act against the universal tendency to be selfishly assertive. Perhaps I should again emphasize that this does not necessarily mean that principles are 'hard-wired' or an inevitable consequence of our genetic make-up. It implies only that human beings or human groups, living in practically any circumstances in which they are viable, are highly likely to develop these characteristics.

Principles are ubiquitous because they are necessary for the integrity of any society, while precepts are part of a complex that contributes to the structure of particular societies and may or may not be observed in other societies. Although precepts may differ between societies, most are compatible with the principle of the Golden Rule. The distinction between principles and precepts is, however, a fuzzy one: precepts may become so much part of human nature in individuals brought up in a stable culture that they are essential to it and have become indistinguishable from principles. 'Do not lie' and 'Do not steal' are examples that have virtually become principles.

Morality has been defined as a series of proscriptions of selfishly assertive behaviour[156]: for most people, however, the proscriptions are linked to prescriptions – instructions that one should be positively prosocial, kind to others, give to charities, and so on – though these are less often stated. Prosociality implies the concept of Virtues, though as abstractions these are perhaps less easy to grasp. The number of virtues that are specified varies, usually between four and seven, the number differing between cultural traditions: generally accepted are Prudence, Justice, Restraint, Courage, Faith, Hope and Charity. They imply goals: thus charity is usually used nowadays to describe benevolent giving to help those in need, but often implies that the giving is accompanied by sympathy or love. Thus, rather than regarding morality as a series of do's and don'ts, it may often be more useful to conceptualise morality in terms of intentions, and beyond that in terms of values, goals or virtues. Thus we all have in some degree a tendency to dominate others, but most of us would value a more peaceful and harmonious society, and recognise that the way towards that is to promote a more egalitarian society. It must be said, however, that the more abstract the terms in which morality is described, the less effective it may be, for 'justifications' may be easier to find.

Our present moral values have served us so far. In the following chapters I refer to some further background issues and matters of emphasis that will be necessary if we are to build more equitable and harmonious societies. In a nutshell, that means societies composed of individuals with a different outlook on the world, individuals whose concern with their own real and supposed needs is diluted by a focus on the good of the community and who see that that means considering the good of all individuals in the society – and ultimately all those outside it. The overall requirement is to build societies that are not dominated by the self-interests of individuals. That may sound like a plea for extreme socialism, but the communist experiment has been shown not to work for just that reason – self-interest and power differentials were still too potent but insufficiently recognised. We need a society of individuals who hold the general good, in a proper proportion to individual needs and desires, as a desirable and achievable aim.

Inevitably, and contrary to my aim to concern the discussion with morality at the individual level rather than with politics or economics, some of the issues that I propose will trespass on the social sciences: their dialectical relations with morality are unavoidable.

The rest of this chapter concerns four basic issues concerning the nature of morality.

Do not ditch all the old
We must seek a morality that is culturally acceptable and fits our changing circumstances, but at the same time we must remember that our culture is shaped by the moral code that we have: we must respect the morality that has served us so far, but be prepared on occasion to adjust or extend it for our current circumstances in the light of our growing knowledge of how people behave and have behaved. The suggestion that a moral code depends on value judgements whose bases can never be available for study so that a rational approach is irrelevant, is based on a superficial view. It is also a council of despair. Instead I have referred to our present knowledge of the evolution of morality and the ways in which morality changes (chapter 3).

Our morality, largely formed by the dialectic between what people do and what they are supposed to do, must be acceptable to the members of the society. While there may be issues over which it is necessary to emphasize some values for the sake of a vulnerable section of society, although those values seem intolerable to others, such problems will become less significant if the good of the community is given a higher priority by all.

Independence from religious belief
As argued in chapters 2 and 4, a new morality must be independent from religious *belief*. Religions have both good and bad consequences for their adherents, and most of the bad ones depend on *beliefs* or *differences in belief*: if what you believe is the *Truth*, other beliefs must be wrong. Differences in belief have been the source of, or justification for, an enormous amount of conflict and suffering. The pronouncements of religious leaders are seen as authoritative, and this has exacerbated conflict between religions and between sects, as well as causing personal suffering.

This does not mean that a religious perspective has nothing to contribute. We have seen that religiosity can have positive consequences for some as well as harm for others. Papal pronouncements reach an enormous audience and Pope Benedict XVI's encyclical calling for global economy oriented towards achieving the common good rather than total wealth is important for us all, though the difficulty is knowing (and agreeing) how to achieve it[32,36,120]. On the other hand, the ambivalent attitude of a previous Pope to Nazism was deplorable, the Catholic ban on contraception has had very adverse consequences on the global problem of over-population, and the mass fundamentalist religions trade on individual salvation rather than the common good. And religion can easily be misused: when Lloyd Blankfein, the head of a major bank, explains away the excessive profits and bonuses of bankers by describing himself as 'doing God's work', something is clearly amiss.

We have seen that the evolution of morality and its development in individuals can be understood in terms of known processes of biological evolution and psychological development. Understanding that our morality has not been imposed by a deity but is something that has been created by humans so that they can live in harmonious societies will make it accessible and acceptable to many twenty-first century minds who doubt any form of theism.

However, for some who do not accept a religious doctrine, some components of religion, like religious ritual or religious music, may nevertheless facilitate prosocial behaviour. This may be a continuing consequence of the way in which religiosity has been part of, and indeed central to, our culture. I have therefore suggested (chapter 2) that our attitude to religion should be carefully selective: the anti-theists are wrong if they want to eradicate it now, though a time may come when that would be appropriate. Religion must certainly not be seen as validating morality by association, or as having priority over humanism in the life of the country.

In a state that contains citizens from many cultural traditions and religious faiths, there is no longer any justification for one religion being specified as the state religion. There are of course understandable reasons why that has come about, and the forces of antidisestablishmentarianism are strong, but they should no longer carry weight. Some revisions in traditional ceremony would (perhaps sadly) be necessary, but they would be in the interests of cultural unity. One cannot expect people of integrity, brought up in one religious tradition, readily to switch allegiance to another. We expect all citizens to have common moral values, but not necessarily a common religion. What is important for societal well-being is moral uniformity, and I have argued that morality is independent of religiosity. Perhaps allegiance to common moral principles could be incorporated into our ceremonial?

For religions represented in authoritarian regimes, special problems may arise. In China the state claims control of the Church, and this has led to conflict with the Vatican: state-appointed bishops have not been recognised by the Pope. China's 10 million Catholics must choose between devotion to the Pope or to state authorities.

Authority
In the past, the good behaviour of citizens has been fostered largely by the possibilities of Heaven or Hell in a later life, aided by the Law. If our future morality is to be independent of religion, it must forgo religion's rewards and punishments. That will not matter provided the necessary incentives and brakes become part of human nature (chapter 10). Righteous indignation by our peers can take the place of threats of Hell, the approval of our fellows can act as incentives. In hunter-gatherers absence of overt conflict is maintained by these forces, but their effectiveness has become diluted by the size and complexity of modern societies. At present, the expression of righteous indignation is suppressed by fear of being seen as self-righteous or hypocritical, and seeking for the approval of one's peers can be seen as a sign of weakness. It is necessary to take a more balanced view, restoring righteous indignation at the aberrant behaviour of one's fellows, and pride in their approval, to more appropriate places in our values.

The possibility of disapproval by one's fellows implies an ongoing state of tension in the group. Over time, as the prevailing world-outlook changes and more communal norms become embedded in peoples' self-systems, we could hope for a reduction in this tension (p. 32-33).

An absolute or a flexible morality?
A moral code must be universally acceptable and moral principles and precepts must be seen as absolute. In apparent contradiction to this, a moral code must have some limited flexibility, for the moral problems with which individuals are faced are seldom simple, and may demand accommodation. The complexity of our societies results in a host of problems in which moral rules that are generally recognized in the society seem to conflict. For instance, who has not felt that to 'bear false witness' might be the moral thing to do because it would avoid someone's unhappiness? Again, one may feel that one should help another who is sick or disabled, but to do so might affront the other's self-esteem. Or it is immoral to steal, but would it be immoral to steal a drug that was otherwise unobtainable if it would save one's wife's life? In retail shops and mail-order operations loyalty to the firm may conflict with scrupulous truthfulness to the customer (see p. 57-60).

Flexibility is necessary also to strike a proper balance between controlling and accommodating to changes in society. As I have stressed, times change and values change. Moral aims must be to some degree congruent with the society, and society with the moral values. The necessity for flexibility should not surprise Jews, Christians or Muslims, for the Old Testament is after all a history of change. St. Paul's letters pointed out the need for change in the way in which people then lived.

Some flexibility will inevitably come from the mutual influences between what people do and what they are supposed to do. It may even be necessary for rules that are good for society to have some let-out: I have mentioned situations in which infanticide is permitted on the grounds of maternal vulnerability (p. 52-53). But there lies the danger, emphasized in chapter 6, that the demands of institutions will lead to perceived situational differences in the applicability of moral values.

Summary
This chapter focuses on the need to find a morality compatible with the world we would like to live in, a morality independent of religious belief but using propensities inherent in human behaviour to control individuals' behaviour, and perceived as absolute but with the possibility of flexibility to cope with changes in society that are compatible with basic moral principles.

8

Social Living: Rights and Responsibilities

In the USA and UK 80-90% of the population live in cities, the citizens meeting every day many people whom they do not know as individuals. This is a very different situation from that in which early humans evolved. In this chapter I suggest that that may be responsible for some of our problems. What is seen as success nowadays depends on the ability to use modern ways of thinking and modern technologies: all children pass through an educational system designed to help them to 'succeed': whether they are taught the most important things is an open issue. And to enable people to retain some individuality in the faceless multitude and to ensure some independence from the power of despots, certain Human Rights are recognised. Unfortunately, in the West it is often forgotten that Rights imply Responsibilities.

Social living and personal development

Urban living has become the norm for most people largely because the opportunities are greater in the towns than in the countryside, it is the way to 'get on'. But the nature of the early environment can have profound effects on development, physical and psychological. For example, the human eyeball becomes longer during childhood, and the evidence suggests that the rate of growth is controlled by the point of focus on the retina. As a result, children reared in the open countryside, with no requirement to read, focus on objects close by much less than urban dwelling children who have much less exposure to open spaces. The urban-reared children are much more likely to become short-sighted[18].

More important in the present context, the incentives of urban living can cause the balance between selfish assertiveness and prosociality to swing beyond our individual psychological capacities to control it. 'Having' has become more important than 'Being'; unbridled competitiveness is too often seen as a prime virtue. Connections to families and groups have become more tortuous and remote as we make our own way in the world, and society has become more individual-oriented. With dense urbanisation, children become less cooperative[68]: such data suggest that we should pay more attention to social development and the development of personal relationships.

Social Living

For urban living to be fully successful we need both the ability to *understand* our fellow human beings at more than a superficial level, and we need a stronger sense of community and of responsibility for the well-being of all its members.

All children develop a 'theory of mind', that is the ability to understand that the behaviour of others is governed by intentions, by the age of about four[14]. But we need more than that: we need to be able to *understand* others. Mutual understanding embraces the concepts of 'interpersonal perception' and 'empathy'. Interpersonal perception involves cognitive issues: for instance, consider the relationship between two individuals, A and B. We can ask whether each perceives the other as similar to her(him)self (Does A see B as similar to how A sees A?); do they understand each other (Does A see B as B sees B?); and does each feel understood (Does B feel that A sees B as B sees B?); with, of course, similar questions for B. 'Empathy' emphasizes the emotional side of inter-personal perception, the extent to which individuals share the pain of another's suffering, or the joy at the sight of another's happiness. For intimate relationships we need to encourage more trust, intimacy, and so on[83, 84, 166]. Understanding another includes understanding his/her motives, and this could in some cases lead to hostility. Thus understanding must be coupled with an ability to act in a way conducive to reducing possible conflict.

Understanding how to enhance the quality of interpersonal relationships is perhaps the most important and the most difficult problem facing humankind and certainly not a matter to be summarised in a few paragraphs. I will not attempt to enter further into that field, but limit myself to a statement that is something more than mere speculation. Early relationships influence the characteristics of later relationships[24]. A capacity for mutual understanding probably develops as a sequel to an upbringing characterised by sensitive loving care and reasoned discipline, augmented by discussion between child and caregiver of particular situations as they arise (p. 44).

But there is an immediate and obvious problem: individual self-assertiveness, doing the best for oneself, is part of human nature and cannot be disregarded. Now the goals towards which self-assertiveness is directed are widely different across societies and across individuals within societies. Some goals are common to individuals in virtually all societies, especially those goals directly connected with reproduction, and some are indirectly but functionally connected with reproduction, like social dominance. But goals connected with reproduction can take curious forms: psychiatrists are only too ready to trace relations between sex and the goals of artistic expression and appreciation. And many find expression for their self-assertiveness in ways that can hardly be connected to reproductive goals: the passion with which the ornithologist pursues the sight of a rare bird, the hours spent on delicate carving to get a four-masted ship into a bottle; the willingness of many fans to queue for hours in the rain to see their favourite football team play.

Since goals are almost infinitely variable we can conclude that they must be labile. We have seen (chapter 5) that there are societies that owe their very nature to the fact that their members direct their self-assertiveness towards maintaining an egalitarian society. An egalitarian society requires individuals who see an egalitarian society *as desirable for themselves* and are prepared to direct their self-assertiveness to achieving it, even at some cost to themselves. I suggest that we must learn from that. A perfectly egalitarian society is certainly beyond our reach, and may not be desirable, but it must be given much higher priority as a goal than it gets at present.

Already we have many NGOs dedicated to improving the world, like Greenpeace, Amnesty and Medécin sans Frontières. Such organisations depend for support primarily on individuals who will not themselves profit from them, and therein lies hope for the future. In addition we need small, perhaps local, groups in which every member can feel responsible for the whole. A focus on the good of all is a proper antidote to selfishness. It is all too clear that our own personal interests are tending to take absolute priority over those of the community, and we need to put more emphasis on the latter than we do.

Both mathematical modelling of society[26, 27] and the example of modern small-scale societies[21] show that a healthy respect for the good of the community requires sanctions against anti-social behaviour: there must be at least some individuals willing to punish those who display too much self-assertiveness. Although tolerance of the idiosyncracies of others is often seen as a virtue, it must have limits: to a certain extent, intolerance of the excessive self-assertiveness of others should be encouraged. Of course, prosociality is also necessary for the well-being of society. It is thus a matter of keeping the propensities inherent in human nature in a better balance: as we have seen, this is the task of morality.

Education

We have seen (chapter 3) that individuals who grow up in homes where they receive sensitive loving care coupled with gentle and appropriate discipline are those most likely to be prosocial with their peers, secure in themselves and thus able to contribute to building more egalitarian societies. Hopefully, they will regard the needs of the community as well as their own. But that also requires encouraging good parenting, and since parenting skills are acquired in part by observation (Note 10), education from outside the family starts at a disadvantage if family sizes are limited to the modern norm. In addition, currently education is inevitably directed largely to teaching people how to succeed in the competition for jobs. Somehow, amongst society's needs, room must be found for education about the nature of personal relationships and, most especially, education that must emphasize the values and the goals of parenthood. This is especially important because the nature of society is changing and future parents, especially young men, need help in understanding children's needs and the responsibilities of parenthood. (Of course human societies can take many forms, but I am considering the form at present prevalent in the West.)

In the past individual needs and social conventions have been allowed to dictate parenting styles, resulting in adverse obstetric techniques, a prejudice against breast feeding, the unnecessary use of wet-nurses, the confinement of children to the nursery, and so on. For at least some of the time, the boot should be on the other leg, with the child's needs dictating societal conventions[97].

Education must also foster a greater consciousness that the goals of an harmonious society must be seen to include everyone's interests, and also the means to achieve them. A better society must be seen not as a pipe dream of academics but as an achievable goal whose realisation is in the interests of every individual. This will require sensitivity, for the goal of an harmonious society must be seen not as dictated by authority, but a desideratum of every individual.

Good parenting and the desire for more egalitarian societies are most likely to be achieved if parents are not burdened by poverty or distracted by riches, in other words if they live in a more egalitarian society of the type we are trying to create.

Human rights and responsibilities

Most societies recognise certain Human Rights. The supposedly definitive Universal Declaration of Human Rights was issued by the United Nations in 1948. It is unnecessary here to refer to the content of its 30 Articles, as they are almost second nature to most westerners. It has, however, one deficiency that is demonstrated by comparison with its Islamic equivalent.

The Universal Islamic Declaration of Human Rights was issued by the Islamic Council in 1981. The preamble of the Islamic Declaration states that it '… is based on the Qur'ān and the Sunnah and has been compiled by eminent Muslim scholars and representatives of Islamic movements and thought'. It has frequent references to the Islamic holy books and assumes that morality should be absolute and unchanging: it can therefore be challenged as out of date. Though broadly similar to the UN document, it has frequent references to Muslim beliefs and differs in a number of respects from the UN statement. This has led to considerable controversy, especially over the rights of women in Islamic countries and the laxity of sexual morality in the West. I do not intend to enter that debate, but one difference between the UN document and the Islamic declaration is highly significant in the present context: the Islamic Declaration emphasizes not only the Rights of individuals but also their Duties. For instance it mentions the duty to protest against injustice, to defend the Rights of others, to protest and strive against oppression, to search after truth and to respect the religious feelings of others. It also gives the poor entitlement to a share in the wealth of the rich, insists that the community has a duty to look after orphans and insists that all means of production should be utilised in the interests of the community.

The Universal (UN) Declaration has virtually no reference to the individual's duties to society. This perhaps reflects the circumstances in which it was compiled, just after the defeat of three authoritarian regimes in World War Two. There are very general references to duties in Article 1 of the UN Declaration (Everyone 'should act towards one another in a spirit of brotherhood') and Article 29 ('Everyone has duties to the community in which alone the free and full development of his personality is possible'), but the duties are left undefined. The UN Declaration is not, indeed should not be, related to any particular religion or to religion in general, but the obligatory relation between rights and duties is surely essential in any society. And it is emphasized in many Christian sources (e.g The Common Good: Catholic Bishops' Conference of England and Wales (undated[32]).

The omission of adequate mention of responsibilities from the UN Declaration is regrettable. Rights cannot exist without responsibilities. For an harmonious society, every citizen should be conscious of the benefits received from the status of a citizen, and recognise that they, by enjoying those benefits, carry responsibilities (Note 11). Reciprocally, of course, society has the duty to ensure that individuals have the opportunity to exercise their rights.

Like moral precepts, 'Rights' are usually seen as unchangeable, or 'inalienable' as the American Constitution puts it. This leads to difficulties. The Second Amendment of the United States Constitution (1791) contains these words:

> *A well regulated Militia being necessary to the security of a free State, the right of the people to keep and bear arms shall not be infringed.*

Abundant evidence indicates that the widespread availability of weapons is a major factor in the high rate of homicide in the United States, yet the perceived authority of the Second Amendment is used by interested parties to preserve the present situation. This continued reverence for the Second Amendment illustrates the dangers in a failure to recognise that times change. In this case financial considerations are involved, and the 'gun lobby' has considerable political leverage.

Other problems arise with the so-called 'Right to Personal Autonomy' which is properly justified in some contexts as a means for protecting individuals from others of higher status, but is an inevitable source of conflict between parent and the maturing child. In addition, autonomy is necessary for the individual's sense of being a unique person and a free agent[119] yet it may conflict with the duties inherent in personal relationships, with group loyalties and duties to society[84].

External threats can lead to bending the rules. The Geneva Conventions for prisoners of war laid down strict rules on prisoners' Rights and how they should be treated. However, the destruction of the Twin Towers on September 11th 2001 led to the use of the US Guatanamo detention camp for suspected terrorists, some of whom have been kept for years without trial. The use of the most devastating forms of torture for extracting information were said to be justified by the belief that further attacks on the USA could be prevented[127]. Freedom of speech, opinion, movement have come to be seen as essential, but it is not always recognised that it becomes logically necessary to grant the same rights to others. In the UK recently steps taken to enhance 'national security' after the terrorist attacks in London have come into conflict with the Right to personal autonomy.

This conflict between the need for moral rules and human rights to be absolute and yet at the same time to have some flexibility has no general solution. In the end, it would seem, any deviation from the rules must be entrusted to the wisdom of a body whose judgments are generally accepted as authoritative. Such a body is not always easy to find, but a precedent exists in the International Court of Justice. The Court has ruled against the threat or use of nuclear weapons except in self-defence when the survival of the state is at stake: on the latter issue the Court was divided.

Individualism and collectivism
These two concepts, while not academically respectable, are useful in discussion of trends in our societies. At present, western societies seem to be steered by selfish assertiveness, self-interest and greed, in other words, to be becoming increasingly individualistic. This individualism of western societies involves a focus on the individual, to the neglect of the group or society. The Christian rationale for 'good' behaviour is often seen as lying in its consequences for the individual rather than the group. In the Sermon on the Mount good behaviour leads to good outcomes for the individual: 'Blessed are the merciful, for they shall obtain mercy'(Matthew, 5, 7). Generalising, one can say that the balance between regard for consequences on the actor and consequences on the group is loaded in favour of the former in the West. A new morality should have a greater regard for the community than we have at present.

I should emphasize that I am not saying that Christianity as practised has no regard for others, or that it is a predominantly selfish religion: on the contrary it abounds with admonitions to help others, to be charitable and so on. In civic life honours go to members of the military but too seldom to philanthropists who give precedence to the community or group over themselves. The point being made is that too often behaviour is motivated by personal profit or salvation, not a communal good. Some reformers in the Islamic world see Islam as in danger of being contaminated by western individualism and the associated western decadence.

The idea that a society could be composed entirely of individuals interested solely in their own welfare and happiness is a contradiction in terms: it simply could not exist. Nor, for different reasons, could a society composed solely of entirely unselfish, cooperative individuals: it would fall prey to outside forces and, anyway, people are just not like that and never will be. It is evident that so far we have failed to find an adequate compromise. Can we do better?

Evidence is accruing that, even amongst western societies, those containing many sub-groups tend to have fewer internal tensions and more trust than those of a similar size whose members seldom meet socially. Such groups can, by increasing interpersonal understanding, reduce tensions in the society as a whole. We need to invigorate the smaller groups within our society, thereby enhancing our 'social capital' (Note 12). Unfortunately, in the USA, and probably elsewhere, the small scale societies and groups that provided experience for all their members in voting and direct decision-making, like churches and community groups, have been declining for over 30 years. We need especially 'bridging social capital' that fosters links between such intra-societal groupings[122,145].

Summary
Modern living requires that that we should be able to form constructive relationships, and achieve real understanding and empathy with our peers. This could be facilitated by adjustments to our educational system, and especially education for parenthood. The privilege of living in a society in which human rights are recognised implies also responsibilities to our peers and to that society. Reciprocally, society must provide the conditions in which individuals can exercise their rights. The well-being of the society must be seen as benefiting individuals and thus as a goal of individuals and not merely of the collective.

9

Social Structures

This book is not about politics or economics, but the dialectical relations between how we behave and how society is organised require comment on some issues at that level. First, if resources are limited, looking after one's own interests inevitably means that individuals compete with each other, and in a competition someone must lose. Competition brings some benefits to the community, but also many problems. Can the intensity of competition be reduced and its evil effects ameliorated? More importantly, can its influence outside the marketplace be confined? Second, the vast discrepancies in wealth in our societies are responsible for much suffering, so they must be reduced. Third, as another consequence of the complexity of our societies, institutions have arisen, apparently for the good of all. But the incumbents of positions in those institutions become governed by their duty to the institution and live in a moral world that is often at variance with their everyday life. Finally, we have seen that prosociality arose in the context of competition between groups, and we are less likely to behave prosocially to members of groups other than our own: for a peaceful world, relations with members of other groups must be more prosocial than they are at present.

Competition

Capitalism is endemic in most western societies and it may or may not be the best way to manage our affairs, but it must not be allowed to justify any sort of behaviour. Capitalism implies competition, a direct consequence of the selfish assertiveness inherent in human nature (see p. 57). We have seen that excessive competition has undesirable consequences (chapter 4). But if competitiveness is part of human nature, it will always be there. Individuals who lacked all selfish assertiveness would be little more than cabbages. However, we can try to provide developmental circumstances that will reduce the precedence at present given to selfish assertiveness in the moral balance (see p. 34).

At the governmental level, it must not be assumed that competitive capitalism is a god whose dictates must be followed at all costs. And it must not be assumed that increasing competition will automatically increase efficiency and the well-being of all concerned. British railways were split into local companies in the belief that competitive bidding for the franchises would reduce prices and increase efficiency. From the passenger's point of view the result has been a reduction in efficiency. A train journey in the UK may require two or three tickets from separate companies for a single journey. If the train on one line is late so that a connection is missed, it is unlikely that either company will accept responsibility. And only rarely does the passenger have choice of carriers.

While my aim is not to argue for one way or another to administer large enterprises, it is necessary to emphasize the importance of the morale of the workers. One had the feeling, and I write only as an outside observer, that the employees of British Rail were proud of being part of an enterprise that was serving the greater community. Comparable feelings in the employees of the local networks are hard to discern. To take another example, a serious problem arose from the inadequate cleanliness of UK hospitals. The response of most hospitals was to employ an external cleaning company rather than their own. Had anything been done to raise the morale of the in-house cleaners? Could they see themselves not as the bottom rung of an unclimbable ladder but as contributing to a great national institution? For external cleaners it is likely to be seen as just another job.

We cannot eliminate competitiveness but surely we could take steps to ameliorate the consequences of excessive competition, some of which were described on p. 57-61. Yet one seldom hears even discussion of how those consequences could be ameliorated. The inversion of the Golden Rule in the commercial world leads to dishonesty: the merits of their products are exaggerated by manufacturers and retailers. This could be reduced by firmer control of advertising, especially media advertising, which should be limited to a statement of how far the product is fit for purpose. We already limit the content of cigarette advertising in spite of the howls of protest from the manufacturers, and the principle could be extended.

The encouragement of consumerism could be countered by differential rates of Value Added Tax, which should be minimal on essential items and greatly increased on luxury items: this principle is already used to raise revenue and reduce alcohol consumption. A similar device could be used to conserve items potentially in danger from excessive exploitation.

The climate of 'Buy now Pay later' could be ameliorated by linking the paying power of credit cards to resources – a course that must surely be technically possible though it would evoke cries of 'nanny state'.

More basic is the need for a change of heart in many of the stakeholders in the marketplace. Short-term self-interest must be replaced by some consideration for the community. Most important is the realisation that over-consumption now and the failure, so far, of nations to curb global warming will have totally unacceptable consequences for those who are young and for the grandchildren of us all. Self-assertiveness will always be with us, but must not be allowed to rule.

Outside the commercial world, capitalistic competition is tending to take control of our lives. I have already stressed how this is happening, and I can only add that it must be resisted. We must guard against the insidious spread of the principles of economic competition into personal relationships: friendships can be ruined by competitiveness. Relationships may depend on exchange (p. 37-40), but social exchange is not the same as economic exchange[20]. In the latter the expected return is usually specified in advance and involves attempts to gain the greatest possible advantage by both sides. In personal relationships the return expected is unspecified and often diffuse. If A does B a good turn he creates a diffuse expectation for reciprocation without specifying what would be fair exchange. Furthermore the consequences for B are as important as those to A for the continuation of the relationship. Trust should not be in doubt.

On the television, games of luck, skill or knowledge depend on monetary rewards: often the losers are dismissed in shame in the full glare of the spotlights. In many cases, competition is inevitable, but it is sad that financial issues are so often central. Football is played largely for monetary rewards. Even cricket, a game in which it is difficult to cheat, has had players who cheated for monetary rewards. In the Oxford and Cambridge Boat Race the winning crew get medals and the losers are seen on television around the world to be dismissed with a hand-shake, although the sacrifices they have made in training may not differ between the two crews. It need not be like that. A shining example is the London Marathon where not only the winner but also all who finish within a certain time get a medal. In the Eisteddfod every choir wants to be judged the best, but there is pleasure in singing whether or not you are in first place. Again there is an informal community of climbers who climb Munros (peaks over 3000 feet in Scotland) and enjoy discussing the Munros they have climbed, with how many they have conquered being a secondary issue. Competition is intrinsic to most of our recreational activities, but the emphasis can be more on taking part, not exclusively on winning. In a recent cricket Test Match, the Indian team decided that a decision that favoured them was unfair, and insisted that it be reversed: a wonderful example of the refrain from the old song – 'The game is more than the player of the game'.

Importance of equality
It is difficult to imagine a form of capitalist society that did not lead to differences between those who have more and those who have less, yet a large gap between rich and poor makes it more difficult to sustain a sense of security and solidarity, and the evidence cited in chapter 4 shows that, in developed countries, income inequality is related to many of society's ills. There is a lesson to be learned from the diversity of the correlates of income inequality. At present each problem is seen as requiring special treatment: low life expectancy is seen to demand better health services; a rise in crime is seen to indicate a need for more police on the beat and more prisons (though prisons do not do well at rehabilitation); teenage pregnancy is countered by better education and contraceptive availability; obesity indicates that people should be encouraged to take more exercise, change their diet, and so on. But each of these problems is related to income inequality. Thus an important step towards a fairer and happier society could lie in the reduction of income inequality: even if the health problems of the poor were ameliorated with first-class health and social services, most of the other problems associated with income inequalities would remain. Major progress towards a healthier and happier society could be expected if the inequalities were reduced.

The goal of social equality denies individual differences, which are inevitable. So what does one mean by equality? There has been a great deal of discussion amongst philosophers and economists about the nature of the inequality that should be considered, but to an outsider the argument seems remote from the real world and merely to confuse the issues[124]. I propose not to enter that debate, and shall consider greater income equality as a goal in competition with other desiderata[164]. This is clearly a political matter, but while politicians may welcome a more equal society in principle, they seem unlikely to promote the major changes that would be necessary in the long run.

The diversity of the problems that would be ameliorated if income differentials were reduced is not appreciated. Many different issues are involved in preventing change: the rising inequality in the USA has been ascribed to the weakening of trade unions, to the influence of the political right, and to changes in taxes and benefits[107]. The inequalities are partly due to the excessively high salaries paid to Chief Executives of major enterprises, especially the trans-national corporations, where those at the top earn many times, sometimes hundreds of times, more than the lowest paid workers. Trades unions were formerly an important corrective to wide income differentials, but governments in both the UK and USA have sought to limit their power and, as I write, the *New York Times* reports that lawmakers in many US States are seeking ways to ban or further limit the power of trades unions. Perhaps worst of all, too often it is the rich who make the rules and the rich who determine public opinion through the media.

The unacceptable differences between rich and poor are a matter that could be ameliorated politically by adjusting tax rates and other regulations. As I have stressed already, not withstanding the dicta of Adam Smith, the rigidity of short-term reciprocity must be ameliorated by some consideration for the long-term well-being of the community. Mechanisms for controlling the inheritance of wealth must be strengthened so that there is a stronger brake on the accumulation of wealth differentials over the generations.

The extent of the influence of inequality in terms of health and happiness seems to be largely a matter of perceived control. Employees who have a feeling of autonomy because they have a degree of control over their work are least affected by income differentials. Especially beneficial are cooperative enterprises where the employees own the company and participate in its management. The John Lewis Partnership and Scott Bader are excellent examples of this principle. In the Scott Bader Commonwealth Ltd management is not responsible to external shareholders, and decisions on the proportion of profits to be put back into the company is in the hands of the workers, or their representatives, themselves. Employee ownership produces a sense of responsibility towards the organisation and, hopefully, to society as a whole. In such enterprises the workers are likely to agree that, in view of the responsibility carried, the executives should be paid more than the workers, but not dozens or hundreds of times more. The membership decides on rates of pay and on the ratio between the highest and lowest (currently 7:1 in Scott Bader). There is evidence that, by various measures of well-being, the influence of such companies spreads into the wider community[69]. It is of interest that the principle of cooperative ownership was endorsed by the Pope in 1961 and 1981, who also exhorted the Roman Catholic Church to cease supporting the more powerful elements in society[120].

It will be apparent that reducing income differences would bring many benefits to society, but the evidence is insufficiently appreciated by politicians whose decisions are improperly influenced by the plutocracy.

Institutions
If we are to build the sort of society we would like, we must dilute the influence of the institutions that lead individuals to behave at variance with their social consciences. People may be constrained to 'bend the rules' because they are called on to do so as incumbents of the roles that they occupy in institutions within our society. So in addition to helping parents to be 'good parents', in addition to reducing poverty and inequality and removing other forces that oppose well-being, we must also ask whether the institutions of our society are to blame (chapter 4). Is the damage they cause justified by the good that they do for society? Can the damage be limited? Our society increasingly promotes individualism and we are losing our sense of community and social responsibility. Is virtually unrestrained capitalism really in our interests? Is our security best preserved by military might?

The marketplace
Given the perceptions of Adam Smith, it is not surprising that competition is the driving force in the business world. It is likely that it will remain so. The important issue is, can it be tamed? As we have seen, the effects of competition between employees within firms or businesses can be ameliorated in firms that are owned by the employees and are organised as cooperatives/commonwealths, such as Scott Bader and John Lewis (p. 100). There is hope that the principles used in these firms will spread to other firms simply because they work well and have succeeded in the competitive marketplace.

The question of monitoring commercial competition between companies is a top-level matter for economists (Stiglitz, 2006). Some progress has been made in the regulation of corporations and false accounting has led to gaol sentences. It helps if a firm's officers are personally responsible for the decisions they make and if firms and/or their officers can be made to pay for damage done. Firms should be responsible to all stakeholders, so that it should be seen as proper for environmental considerations to lead to a reduction in shareholders' dividends. Regulations about the quality of goods and against built-in obsolescence are possible, but very difficult to enforce. But these are all top/down matters and beyond the scope of this book. What is required is a change in the world-views of both managers and individual consumers.

The financial system entails the view that people are greedy, and that perpetuates the situation. We have a market economy, and economists are only slowly realising that people are not wholly greedy (see p. 30). Many, perhaps most, people prefer dealings to be fair – though what counts as fair is not always clear: as discussed in chapter 3, 'fairness' poses difficult problems. Economists argue that rewards should be proportional to work put in and the risks taken[98] and the market would probably work better that way. But some allowance must be made for the sick, the handicapped, the aged, and the consequences of bad and good luck. Lady Luck may try to distribute her favours equally, but it is the needy who get the short straws.

Encouraging fair dealing may be a matter of self-interest, if only those involved would see it: if an ethic of fair dealing prevails now, I shall not have to worry so much when I next enter the market. But the nature of the market encourages deceit and greed. The gross unfairness in the incomes of bankers, derived from gambling with other people's money without responsibility when they lose, has become public knowledge and a matter of public protest since the 2008 recession. Money changes hands, but the community is not better off. Clearly the banks must be controlled, but what government will take that on? The advantages of worker owned enterprises, such as Scott Bader, where the profits are shared amongst the workers and where the workers have the responsibility of deciding how the business should be run, are not yet fully appreciated.

A possible but very partial solution lies in the great variety of schemes to encourage public sharing that are now appearing[22]. Rationally it is clearly ridiculous for each household in a community to own an electric drill that it will use for perhaps half an hour a month. But unfortunately a (perhaps macho) propensity for possessiveness operates against sharing. Nevertheless many people are learning to pay for what they use rather than what they own. The trend was set by time-sharing schemes: you do not own a holiday house, but contribute to a group that owns a number and you may use one when you want it. Product service schemes are being set up: some towns have set up bicycle sharing schemes which both reduce the exhaust gas pollution from cars and enable people to use a bicycle when they want one. For such schemes to work there has to be enough choice to satisfy users, there must be sufficient stock so that what you want is available when you want it, and there has to be a degree of trust. These and many other systems of collaborative sharing are becoming more frequent.

War
War can be seen as an institution: in preparations for war, or in war itself, the behaviour of individuals is largely governed by the duties associated with the roles they occupy. Not only do the combatants fight in part because it is their duty to fight, but the workers in armament factories, the commanders, the politicians, the medics do what they do in part because of the duties associated with their roles in the institution of war.

Many have believed that war is an inevitable consequence of the human condition. That is a mistake[90]. In time, people will recognise that, in modern war, both sides lose. In addition war is immoral, wasteful, and cruel. International disputes are better settled round the conference table, and not with guns, for violence only breeds more violence. I do not deny that, in today's world, war may sometimes, though rarely, be necessary, but it can legally be started only by, or on behalf of, the United Nations (UN Charter, Articles 2:3 and 2:4). Unfortunately the United Nations, like its predecessor the League of Nations, is handicapped by its Charter from interfering in conflicts within states, and has neither the power nor the structure to be effective in preventing or ameliorating inter-state conflicts. Its lack of resources is another example of selfish individualism at another level of complexity: when it comes to votes on the Security Council or General Assembly countries tend to look after their own interests and the needs of the world are forgotten.

If we are to hasten the day when war is abolished or at least seen as a very last resort, we must work at two levels, the political level, and with the grass roots. In democracies, efforts can be made to influence politicians and to provide them with accurate information on the probable consequences of their decisions, and to act as a go-between in disputes: the International Pugwash organisation and the UK Pugwash Group and other NGO's have had considerable success in this way. Their work depends on maintaining a reputation for impeccable scientific integrity and lack of bias, and they must therefore operate largely out of the public eye. With the general public, a variety of approaches are possible: in Britain the UK Pugwash Group, the Movement for the Abolition of War and other organisations do dedicated work. The task is becoming increasingly difficult as the proportion of people with first-hand experience of war decreases, so convincing the young of its real nature is of special importance[85, 90].

Politics
If democracy is to work, voters must believe that their elected representatives have their interests at heart, and not their own. The not wholly rational tendency of many people in western societies to see politicians as corrupt and self-interested has received considerable support in the UK from the revelation that some Parliamentarians had been fiddling their expenses. Of course politicians are not all corrupt, but it is essential not only that all should be honest and concerned with the general good but also that they should *be seen* to be so. Whether their private life is irrelevant to their public duties is a matter of ongoing debate, but their personal integrity over public matters is of the greatest importance. There is, of course, a two-way relationship here: it is harder for a parliamentarian to be virtuous if the society in which he/she lives is corrupt.

The democratic system itself contains many traps, some almost unavoidable. To get elected a candidate may have to distort his ideals to fit what he perceives the electorate to desire. If a Whip system operates within a party, he may have to vote as his party decrees even if it means sacrificing his integrity: if he does not he may lose party support or his chances of promotion. One wonders how far party loyalty is essential, and whether the Whip system could be diluted? Could lobbyists' attempts improperly to influence policies and the voting of individual members be curtailed?

Individuals are, of course, tempted to put their own interests first, so that voting for reforms that are believed to be in the nation's interests but against those of the individual requires great integrity. A government's ability to contribute to the solution of world problems is severely handicapped by its need to please its voters: the failure of the USA to ratify the Kyoto Protocol on climate change because it was claimed that it would harm the US economy disregarded the longer-term view that not ratifying it will harm our children and grandchildren.

That is one reason why we have morality. Adam Smith argued that self-interest was proper in the market-place, but not in politics. I have argued that there are limits on the propriety of self-interest in the market-place and the case is even stronger for politics. Those who rule must put the common good above their own and consider themselves bound by the laws that bind the electorate. This makes democracy inevitably fragile so that constant vigilance is necessary. A politician's life may be his own, but integrity in all matters related to his work is essential and transparency is necessary.

However, the problem does not lie only with the politicians. The voting public must be attuned to its responsibilities, including the responsibility to vote in elections. It has been argued that a democracy, to be successful and to ensure the involvement of its members, must embrace groups that practise 'direct democracy', where all the members of the group vote on every issue. It would be impossible for all citizens in a parliamentary democracy in a large state to vote on every issue, but the existence of smaller groups within the society, where the whole electorate of the community could practise direct voting, enhances responsibility to vote in parliamentary elections. Direct democracy could facilitate a sense of community involving friendships that create trust between individuals and makes it possible for individuals to accept differences of opinion and compromises. The existence of smaller groups within the society which help to build up 'social capital' does in fact benefit the well-being of the citizens[122].

Religion
Churches are clearly aware of their own internal problems and it is unnecessary to comment. But, in Christian churches, a change in emphasis from 'belief' to 'morality' and a greater emphasis on responsibilities to the community rather than the self would, by the arguments presented here, clearly be desirable.

Xenophobia and cultural differences
In some respects we must work towards a world that is contrary to our biological nature. We have seen that the evidence suggests that prosociality evolved in the context of inter-group competition and

rivalry: those groups whose members helped each other were more likely to succeed in competition with other groups and its members were more likely to be reproductively successful and to pass on their moral outlook by cultural or genetic selection. In terms of the prosociality/selfish assertiveness model (p. 34), behaviour towards members of the same group will involve both prosociality and selfish assertiveness, while behaviour to outsiders would be characterised only by selfish assertiveness. Although this situation was shaped when each group consisted of only a few families, it still influences our behaviour today. Individuals who are unfamiliar or strange are likely to be seen as outsiders, or at least treated differently from in-group members. This tendency can be exacerbated by religious and language differences, patriotic rivalry or markers that accentuate the differences. It is this that has fostered international competition and war. I believe that, in the western world at least, the situation is improving. People of other races, speaking different languages, with different cultures, are at last coming to be seen as fellow human beings. Globalisation, though it has many problems, is helping to make this a universal feeling. Individuals and countries send aid to alleviate natural disasters wherever they strike.

Xenophobia is fed by differences in culture, and especially in morality, between societies. Societies differ in both ecology and history, and must be expected to have somewhat different value systems. Tolerance for the views of members of other societies is therefore essential and, as we have seen, tolerance tends to be incompatible with strongly held beliefs. It may not (yet?) be possible for all fully to adopt some of the democratic desiderata which the great majority of Westerners (though not everyone) see as self-evident – equality, democracy, adequate privacy, open government. Indeed it is far from clear that an immediate switch to democracy is appropriate for a previously tribal society, or one embracing somewhat contradictory religious beliefs, hitherto held together by an autocrat. However, this does not justify a complete cultural relativism that, if taken to extremes, could be taken to mean that people could subscribe to any values, or even to no values. This is a critically important issue, for there have been societies that have developed codes by which the oppression of some groups was legitimated, or codes that insisted on the rectitude of its own beliefs so rigidly that individuals were encouraged to propagate them by force. In different ways, slaves in American civilisations and in Africa, Jews and gypsies in the Nazi era and the untouchables in India were regarded as virtually non-persons. From the perspective of most outsiders, such codes could not be condoned. All individuals in all societies are human beings, and their needs are similar if not identical.

But problems arise with immigrant populations with strong religious views that conflict with those of the host society. For instance, should immigrants from a culture where polygamy is the norm be allowed to continue the practice in a country where it is seen as immoral and illegal? The wearing of a headscarf by Muslim women in western European countries is seen by some as an element of Islamic ideology and its prohibition as contrary to the principle of religious freedom, while others see it as a symbol of the oppression of Muslim women or as an attempt by Muslim leaders to exercise control independently of the state. We have already discussed the necessity for all citizens of a multi-cultural society to share a common morality, but this need not imply a common system of religious beliefs.

Although differences in religious belief have been causal to war or have facilitated wars, both the UN Declaration of Human Rights and the Universal Islamic Declaration regard freedom of religion as a Human Right. In the main, the troubles arise primarily from differences in *belief*. Thus attempts to understand the nature of religious beliefs are essential (chapter 2): if the beliefs are seen not to be literally true, the problems disappear.

I suggest that disapproval of any culture that did not recognise the full rights of individuals is justified (with certain exceptions such as the insane or criminals who cannot or have not exercised their duty to society) and any culture in which the Golden Rule was not basic. At the same time we should be prepared to learn from any society whose morality seems to fill gaps in our own – as the Chinese apparently learned over foot-binding, and as Westerners might emulate the ethic of communal responsibility as seen in some Islamic and east Asian countries.

In a more detailed discussion elsewhere[84] I have suggested that interaction with someone from a very different culture should start with matters of common interest, like children or food. And one must try to distinguish moral differences that result from the culture and those arising from the behaviour of a particular individual. Of course this does not solve the problems: can one pin all the blame for a genocidal policy on the leader and completely exonerate the camp guard who carries it out?

Globalisation
Globalisation has resulted in many problems formerly seen as local problems becoming world problems, and demanding world solutions. Diseases spread across borders, terrorists trained in one country can cause mayhem in another, climate change demands joint action by all countries, the spread of nuclear weapons is an international problem. Globalisation also has other unfortunate consequences. It has increased the difference between rich and poor both within countries and between countries. Already advances in technology are enlarging the gap between those who can cope with the demand for skills and those who cannot. The migration of workers to take unskilled jobs in the developed countries inevitably creates problems for the unskilled workers in the latter. Some of the problems stem from attempts to impose an American-type political system on countries that are not suited to it, causing resentment amongst the people and even civil war. As I write there is civil war in the Ivory Coast because the President who has been defeated in an apparently fair election refuses to step down: apparently the country was not ready for democracy.

However, we must recognise that globalisation cannot be held back, and governments must think globally and recognise that measures to protect sections of their own economy may have devastating effects in other countries. Rather they must try to redress the lot of the poorer sections of their societies, and do everything possible to improve education so that the proportion of skilled workers is increased, and especially so that the proportion of very skilled innovators is increased. At present, each country pushes its own interests in discussions on trade issues: democracy at the international level is almost absent. International trade agreements are conducted by finance ministers with little regard for the consequences on global warming. The World Bank and the International Monetary Fund do their best, but mistakes are made.

Divisions between nation states are becoming less important, especially in Europe, but globalisation does not call for abolition of nation states – at any rate not for the foreseeable future. But recent events show that an overall supervision of the world economy is needed, and that means one not dominated by the rich countries or by the winners of the last major war. A reformed United Nations might fit the bill.

Summary
This chapter discusses some ways in which culture affects our behaviour that need consideration. The need to reduce competitiveness in everyday life has already been mentioned. If differences in wealth could be reduced, many of society's ills could be ameliorated. Our societies require institutions, but they must not be allowed to pervert our morality. We must come to terms with cultural differences: in this globalisation acts both ways.

10

Building on What We Have

To achieve all the changes outlined in the previous chapters may seem like an impossible task. In this final chapter I emphasize that many of the changes needed for a more harmonious society are not against our nature: a better society could be achieved by accentuating propensities that we already possess.

Righteous indignation
Existing egalitarian societies do not consist of collections of goody-goodies, but of individuals who suppress those who assert themselves inappropriately (p. 68-71). A tendency to put down others who push themselves forward or who disrupt the equilibrium of the group was an essential element in the evolution of prosociality (p. 31-32). In western societies most people feel at least a little uncomfortable if a colleague acts above his station. Introspection shows that the tendency to disapprove of those who seem to be too self-assertive is still present in ourselves, but it is often suppressed by fear of being seen as hypocritical, pretentious or of acting out of turn, or by a feeling that one should not poke one's nose into other people's business, the last perhaps a symptom of individualism. The feeling of righteous indignation when we perceive others to be behaving improperly is probably found in all humans but is not prone to lead to action in our present society. We could do with a bit more righteous indignation when others unjustifiably push themselves forward or break the rules. This does not mean that we should disregard others' expertise, so it demands sensitive judgement about when to disapprove.

My subjective impression, and I have no data to back this up, is that we have much less tendency to show righteous indignation to those with whom we are less closely connected, especially celebs and royalty. Magazines thrive on the minutiae of their dress and behaviour, and especially on news of their wrong-doings. Maybe this is related to the fact that we can do nothing about them anyway.

Righteous indignation can be effective only if others are afraid of eliciting social disapproval. That is indeed the case. How often can one honestly say that one's unsocial actions were autonomous, with no element of fear of disapproval? How often can one say that one was generous with no hope of gratitude? Here I am not down-grading the basic prosociality of individuals, but refer to the social factors that inhibit the opposing characteristic of self-assertiveness so that prosociality can be more generally expressed.

The extreme case in society as a whole is whistleblowing. Whistleblowing must now be seen as an act of great courage, as it usually involves exposing the whistleblower to revenge from someone or some people in a position of power over the whistle-blower. Mordechai Vanunu's courageous exposure of the fact that Israel was secretly manufacturing nuclear weapons with disregard for international agreements led to his being kidnapped by the Israeli security services and savage sentences of 18 years in prison, including 11 years in solitary confinement, followed by restrictions on his movements and contacts.

Another case reported in the press involved a doctor employed by a pharmaceutical firm to promote a drug that had been approved for the treatment of epileptic seizures. He found that he was expected to recommend it also for other complaints and that some of the children treated suffered side-effects, but was ordered not to tell doctors about them. He also encountered other instances of malpractice. When he made this public he suffered seven years of legal wrangling, his career was destroyed and he became a recluse. Eventually the firm was fined $240 million criminal fine and $152 million to state and healthcare authorities. He received $26.6 million: a large sum but poor recompense for what he had suffered (*Independent*, May 15th, 2004).

It is not easy to have the courage to expose wrong-doing, but whistleblowers with a legitimate complaint should be protected from vengeance from those exposed.

Competitiveness

As we have seen, competition leads to tension for all involved and suffering for the losers. I have discussed the question of how to ameliorate the effects of excessive competition in the last chapter.

As I have already emphasized, what is especially regrettable from the present perspective is the extent to which competitiveness is coming to enter into every aspect of our lives – even recreational activities and personal relationships. It need not be so. As stressed already, every one wants to win, but that need not be the only issue. The emphasis can be on taking part, not exclusively on winning.

Gossip

In modern western societies we are bombarded with information about what is going on in the world, but that is little help in guiding our relationships in our own small worlds. However, most people have an intense interest in other people's affairs, though few will own up to it. The space given by the media to reporting crimes indicates that interest in wrong-doing is still potent and sells newspapers. It is of interest that the focus of interest is the bad, rather than the good, things in other people's behaviour. I have already commented on the way in which the media report murders, robberies and so on, and not the prosocial things that people do. This preference for news about evil and wrong-doing could be (and here I speculate with little evidence) a remnant of the role played by gossip in preventing undesirable behaviour in the egalitarian societies likely to have existed amongst our ancestors (p. 68-71).

Gossip, so important in enabling bossiness to be nipped in the bud in egalitarian societies, is a feature of our society, but is seen by many as the province of people who have nothing better to do. The tendencies to gossip about other people's affairs and to show moral indignation are muted: interference in another's behaviour is seen as symptomatic of being a busybody, and that carries a strong pejorative judgement. It plays little part in suppressing overt self-assertiveness.

Could gossip have a role in promoting greater egalitarianism in modern societies? There would have to be a very difficult balance between encouraging some interest in other people's lives and not involving improper invasions of privacy. As I write, hacking into private emails and eavesdropping on private conversations have become standard tools for some journalists, but this is not accepted and has given rise to public indignation and legal prosecutions. Gossiping solely to the advantage of the gossiper should be strongly discouraged, but reporting bad behaviour clearly has a role in building a better society.

Sharing

For all individuals of any society, whether or not egalitarian, sharing resources is desirable just because some individuals are more fortunate than others. We have seen that the sharing of resources that are difficult to obtain plays a central role in modern hunter-gatherer societies (chapter 5).

Sharing becomes imperative if groups are to survive under extreme conditions. In Auschwitz prisoners were forbidden by the authorities to help each other, but almost every survivor had been helped by another inmate at sometime or other[43]. The same was true in the Gulags. An Auschwitz survivor described how stealing bread from another prisoner was regarded as unpardonable and punished by execution. 'If a man stole your food, you killed him; it was rough justice. If you were not strong enough to carry out the sentence yourself, there were other executioners ... it was fair because to deprive a man of food was to murder him.'

But what leads to sharing outside such extreme conditions? One of the most effective forces for inducing sharing amongst the members of a community has been religion. In Christian countries the view that wealth should be shared was clearly recognised in the system of tithes: this obliged citizens to give a proportion of their wealth, originally one tenth, to charity. This has now largely fallen into disuse. As we have seen, the importance of sharing is recognised in the Universal Islamic Declaration of Human Rights, but not in the UN or the Cairo declarations. The Universal Islamic Declaration of Human Rights includes the following in its Article XV:

'The poor have the right to a prescribed share in the wealth of the rich'

and

'All means of production shall be utilised in the interest of the community (Ummah) as a whole, and may not be neglected or misused.'

The concept of sharing is central to the work of charitable organisations, to much of Christ's teaching and to the Muslim ethic. The concept of sharing was basic to the Communist Manifesto of 1848, and during the nineteenth century in western countries there was a growing consciousness of the plight of workers and the unfairness in the distribution of wealth. Quaker Social Action was set up in 1867 to ameliorate the situation, and organisations such as Dr. Barnardo's and the Shaftesbury Homes for destitute young people around the same time. Pope Leo XIII spoke up in 1891 and Pope John XXIII in 1961. From then the Roman Catholic Church has spoken up several times on questions of social justice, and Pope John Paul II emphasized the priority of labour over capital, condemning the extremes of both socialism and capitalism. Some of the institutions of our societies, such as public libraries, public baths and swimming baths, and public transport, are based on sharing, though we do not think of it as such.

There is experimental evidence that a propensity to share fairly is widespread in many societies. Deciding what is fair, however, poses a problem. A basic assumption seems to be that sharing should be equal, and that is illustrated in the "ultimatum game". Individuals are paired randomly but do not meet and have no information about each other. Some money is given to one of them, who is told to share it with the other. The rule is that the recipient must accept his share: if he rejects it, neither is allowed to retain anything. Since the game is played only once, the recipient has no incentive to reject in the hope of being offered a larger slice next time. One might expect the holder of the money to offer as small a share as the recipient is likely to accept and the recipient to accept whatever is on offer. In practice the holder usually offers something only a little short of half of the amount he has been given. Apparently his feeling that equal shares are appropriate partially overrides his selfishly assertive wish to keep as much as he can. Recipients often refuse to take what they are offered if they consider it to be too little[80].

The criteria for fairness in sharing can give rise to problems, for what is fair may depend on the context (see p. 39). Especially dangerous is the widespread assumption that certain characteristics entitle some individuals to privileged treatment. This has been most obvious in the system of hereditary rank in UK society, but that is slowly disappearing. There is a danger, however, that it will be replaced by wealth: wealth brings power and for purely pragmatic reasons, power demands respect. Associated with that is the culture of celebrities. Celeb status may be gained by outstanding prowess in sport, the theatre or what have you, but it becomes enhanced by acolytes who benefit from the association with the celeb's status, and by magazines dedicated to the minutiae of a celeb's existence and feeding an apparently insatiable public readership. Much more reasonable in many contexts is that wealth or celebrity status should be replaced by the need of the recipient or by the contribution he or she has made in providing a resource of value to the community.

The ethic of sharing suffers from the pressures of individualism and materialism. Yet the high membership of organisations like Amnesty, Greenpeace, the Royal Society for the Protection of Birds, the National Trust and other charities of which membership is not solely a matter of self-interest suggests that the impulse to share good fortune is still potent if we look for it. It is even more apparent in the electorate-supported governmental donations in foreign aid and disaster relief.

But nevertheless a focus on maintaining an harmonious society, so central in egalitarian hunter/gatherer societies, is not very apparent in modern societies. The emphasis on the marketplace and the importance of competition point away from an ethos of sharing. Although some concern for universal human welfare has been with us for many years, it is in danger of drowning in the demands of modern life. These demands come from the deadly combination of widespread poverty and the greed even of those whose "needs" are already met.

Individual behaviour and social structure

We have seen that prosociality itself probably evolved through cultural group selection, and at the individual level concerned the importance of ensuring that *other people* should behave prosocially, and thereby that each individual should behave prosocially himself (p. 30-32). Regard for the relative importance of consequences for the actor and consequences for the group differ between individuals and between societies. We have seen that, in most western cultures, people are taught primarily to look after their own interests, at any rate for most of the time: instead we need to build on the propensities that support the integrity and harmony of the group. Perhaps western countries should listen to the Islamic reformers who see Islam as being perverted by western selfishness and individualism.

We differentiate between members of our own group and outsiders. Indeed we create markers of group membership and encourage loyalty to the group, tending to denigrate outsiders. There are both pluses and minuses here, but in the globalised modern world we need to see ourselves not only as members of a local group but also as members of the human species. There is a real problem here, as the world would be poorer for lack of cultural diversity. At the same time, we must learn to value individuals from all cultures equally: there must be no exceptions on the grounds of race, gender, or nationality. This will not be easy, because we are used, especially in times of inter-group competition, to propaganda encouraging denigration and even the destruction of all those outside our own group.

Perhaps the very fact that our aversion to strangers becomes stronger when the strangers are threatening should give us hope. Today the whole human race is threatened by the spread of nuclear weapons and by global warming. The former could result in the destruction of the planet as we know it, the latter could render parts of the planet uninhabitable by destroying ecosystems on which life depends. The problems threaten the whole of humankind, and we must see outsiders to our local group as allies. Both of these dangers could be reduced if individualism and greed could be minimized, if we could learn to understand the needs of our neighbours and act to facilitate a more equitable distribution of resources. Along the way we must learn that unlimited competitiveness must be restrained. None of this means that we should do away with local cultures and aim for a uniform world: we value our human diversity and no one in their right mind could want to live in a uniform hamburger and Coca-Cola world. But the dangers that threaten our planet are so great that we must act together.

The conscience
It was necessary for me to start this book by emphasizing many of the things that are symptomatic of, or act against, an harmonious society, so perhaps it is appropriate to remember those things in our personal behaviour that are conducive to behaviour that could help build the sort of society we would be more comfortable to live in.

We all have a conscience that, in terms of the model I used (p. 34), helps us to behave morally. A discrepancy between the guidelines and values internalised in our self-concepts and our proposed actions leads to attempts to remove the discrepancy (p. 46-47). The values are imparted to the baby, infant or young person by those around him, parents, peers or teachers. Education, not just the teaching of facts, is basic (p. 91). Good role models are important: one may fear dishonour or disappointing a loved one if one does not act cooperatively: even late in life one finds oneself thinking 'What would my parents have thought if …?'. Cultural identification may be important: I was brought up with 'An Englishman's word is as good as his honour.' (In the first chapter I acknowledged that as soon as one starts to discuss these issues, one becomes an easy target for accusations of hypocrisy). We have seen that one's self-concept involves one's environment or community (p. 46-47): it follows that we should be as sensitive to anything that infringes the integrity or quality of that community as we are to discrepancies with our own individual self-concepts. Experience of direct community action on a local scale, membership in a football team, choir, natural history society or stamp collectors club may provide a positive approach to community that becomes incorporated into one's self-concept and informs one's approach to a wider regional or national community. The goal must be an aspiration to build a fairer and more just community.

The example of Japan

At least one modern society, Japan, deserves attention because it is so different from the West yet has some relevant and important characteristics highly relevant to the theme of this book[112]. Eastern ways of thinking are very different from those of western societies in many ways, some quite fundamental. For instance in conflicts between formal and intuitive reasoning, European Americans tend to rely on the former rather than the latter, while Chinese and Koreans rely more on intuitive strategies[117]. This difference is likely to apply to all East Asian countries and underlies differences in philosophies, religion and basic ways of thinking. Japanese society is also very different from the sort of society that many of us would like in that, for instance, it is very hierarchical. But there are two characteristics that are of interest in the present context, the nature of everyday interactions, and the capacity for sharing.

Japan's society seems almost incomprehensible to outsiders. In Japan, sometimes described as a village transported to a city, harmony is the apparent goal of almost all interpersonal behaviour. To the foreigner, interactions and public relationships seem deferential, even defensive and obsequious: people warily avoid any sign of pushiness or aggression, but seem as though trying to ingratiate themselves with each other. 'Tentative harmony, trust, relationality, and desire to please and be pleased, all these are stressed purposes of greeting etiquette'. 'Politeness and etiquette come before morals and before law', and it seems more important to be polite than to tell the truth[112]. In Japan 'Affection is more important than logic or ethics'.

In Japan there is no judging God, nor any polytheistic system of powerful gods who must be placated. Language is used to avoid confrontation, and argument and debate are avoided. The Japanese desire for harmony has even extended to the building, after a battle, of two kinds of shrine, one for the winners of a battle and one for the losers: this is believed to calm down the losers' anger and soothe the negative side of the past. The need to maintain an harmonious atmosphere is deeply ingrained in the Japanese psyche, and the need to put down anyone who is becoming selfishly assertive is described as the 'need to hit the nail flush with the wood'. Even in childhood the fear of being seen as pushy is strongly reinforced both by positive reward and by punishment (or threat of punishment) so that it is incorporated into the self-concepts of individuals and comes to govern every facet of their lives.

This differs only in degree from our own behaviour when we disguise our feelings about our friends or friends' friends for fear of offending them. We follow the rules of politeness not because we fear God's punishment, but ultimately because we fear the disapproval or ridicule of our friends. We are uncomfortable when someone else appears to be acting out of turn or being too self-assertive, but in the West we refrain from comment for fear of being impolite or causing unpleasantness.

New Orleans and Haiti have both suffered major disasters in recent years, and in both cases the disaster was followed by extensive looting. This was not the case in Japan after the triple disasters of earthquake, tsunami and damage to a nuclear power station: little looting occurred, and the people, though desperate for food, still waited in line for groceries. In some of the devastated areas the survivors banded together and began to divide the tasks necessary for their future joint survival – boiling water, scavenging for food and petrol, preparing food. Within at least some areas they established communities, with an impromptu governing body and communication with neighbouring refugee centres. The stoicism and self-sacrifice, the quiet bravery in the face of tragedy, were remarkable to western reporters[60]. Even the organised crime syndicates kept an eye out for looters and provided extensive humanitarian aid, though later they sought to profit from clearing up the mess.

No doubt the difference from New Orleans and Haiti has many causes, including Japan's long history, its isolation, and its tradition of surmounting natural disasters. Those affected in New Orleans and Haiti were mostly the very poor whose lives had previously been a struggle for survival. They had virtually no feelings of community. It is perhaps as a consequence of such differences that the remarkably honest and altruistic behaviour of the Japanese after the disaster seemed to have been part of the Japanese psyche. Not, however, in all individuals: some observers pointed out that the response to disaster would have been very different amongst a younger, predominantly entrepreneural city population where western influences have weakened the traditions. And there are other factors operating to maintain prosociality in Japan. There are rewards for turning in lost property to the police station, and also penalties for failure to turn in property that you have found. There is a strong police presence. In the language I have been using, it seems as though the balance between the propensities for prosociality and selfish assertiveness are traditionally maintained more in favour of prosociality than is usual in the West, and this seems to be due to values embedded in the self-system early in life, aided by fear of social punishment.

The fear of offending in Japan is additional evidence for the model I have been trying to sketch – namely two basic propensities, to develop prosociality and selfish assertiveness, each involving constraints and predispositions to learn, each responsive to experience, and with behaviour that is appropriate according to cultural conventions. Prosocial behaviour is accentuated and appears predominant. But the propensity for selfish assertiveness is still present and responsive to circumstances that could inhibit the prosocial behaviour.

Conclusion

The first response of many readers to the views I have expressed may be 'Idealism!' or 'It is impossible'. To that I have two answers:

The first is that something must be done. It is too easy to accept the world as unfair and as based on self-interest and greed, with the resulting tensions and conflict. It is also too easy to feel that nothing can be done, or that the problem is beyond the concern of individuals. We cannot just sit in our comfortable western homes with no concern for those who starve in the slums of São Paulo or the deserts of sub-Saharan Africa, or for our successors who are likely to inherit a polluted world even less harmonious than our own. We must create a new world outlook based on mutual responsibility in which service to the well-being and smooth-running of our own community and of the community of humankind is seen as an important personal goal. We need to create a sense of mutual responsibility. I know it's easy for someone living in the comfortable West to believe that it is possible to change world outlooks: some will say, just try to get the Palestinian refugees, or those just managing to scrape a life together in the outskirts of a modern metropolis, to understand. The reply must be that we must start at home. It will be a long haul, but we have the potential.

The second answer to the doubters is that the logic is inescapable. I have tried to express it in successive chapters:

Chapter 1.	(a) Our societies are not as harmonious as they could or should be.
(b) This is largely due to individual selfishness, greed or whatever you like to call it.
(c) There are dialectical relations between our political and economic systems and the morality of individuals, with each affecting the other. Therefore, in addition to seeking for better politico-economic systems, we should also start from the bottom and consider the morality that guides individual behaviour.
Chapter 2.	Morality is often seen as related to religion, but religion provides an insecure base for morality in the modern world.
Chapter 3.	The genesis of morality in the course of human evolution can be understood in terms of natural and cultural selection and the changing nature of humankind. The acquisition of morality by individuals is now fairly well understood by developmental psychologists.
Chapter 4.	The morality that is more or less accepted in our societies has specifiable deficiencies.
Chapter 5.	Change is possible.
Chapter 6.	Change, though possible, will be slow and difficult.
Chapters 7, 8 and 9.	The issues on which it will be necessary to focus can be specified. Of special importance are education directed towards strengthening the desire for harmonious communities and the means to achieve them; a willingness to restrain anti-social behaviour in others as well as in oneself, gossip (in moderation) as a means of monitoring behaviour; and a willingness to share.
Chapter 10.	Much of what is required involves only greater emphasis on aspects already present in our psyche.

It is a matter of the greatest significance that the propensities important in maintaining small-scale egalitarian societies early in human history are still present in our own. The problem is that these propensities, to value a peaceful society, to act on moral indignation by punishing overt self-assertiveness, and to share good fortune, are too often seen as old-fashioned. The conclusion too often drawn is that morality is out-of-date, but it is equally possible to see the present organisation of our society as incompatible with what is desirable for an harmonious world. We need to work towards a new world-outlook in which morality involves a greater regard for the community than we have at present. This implies a new outlook on the world in which the well-being and smooth-running of the community is seen as an important goal by each one of us, and within communities individuals value good relations with each other and are discouraged from behaving antisocially. We must work towards a society with its own mechanisms for social control, without dependence (conscious or unconscious) on concepts of Heaven and Hell.

I am not attempting to purvey a new political or economic system, though I believe both will be necessary. Probably a number of such systems to suit different circumstances will be required. But we shall not find them unless we also start at the bottom to try to build a new world-view in individuals such that they are oriented to more communal goals and less towards their own personal interests. Many many people have said this before, but if it is indeed the case that the problem is one of encouraging propensities that we already have, it should not be impossible.

Notes

1. The Roman Catholic Church lists the Seven Deadly Sins (and their antitheses) as follows: Extravagance (including Lust) vs Chastity; Gluttony vs. Temperance; Greed vs Charity; Acedia (Melancholy) vs. Diligence; Wrath vs Patience; Envy vs Kindness and Pride vs Humility. This is the list developed by Pope Gregory I in 590 C. There are other lists. They do not correspond precisely to lists in the Bible (see e.g. Proverbs, 6, 16-19 and Galatians 5, 19-21). A variety of lesser sins are also recognised, such as cruelty, hypocrisy, snobbery, betrayal. Shklar[137] adds dishonesty.
2. Haidt (in Schloss & Murray[130]) considers morality to involve five systems:
   (a) Fairness and Justice. We shall see (p. 39) that defining what is fair itself involves considerable problems: decisions could be seen as involving cognitive reasoning affected by emotional dispositions.
   (b) Harming others and Care for others[65]. Both Fairness/Justice, and Harming/Care as aspects of morality may have originated in the importance of maintaining balance between the two propensities of prosociality and selfish assertiveness. Both are related to the Golden Rule of Do-as-you-would-be-done-by or some variant thereof, which I suggest is basic in all societies, and is indeed essential if a society is to hold together at all (p. 37).
   (c) In-group loyalty. We shall see that this was intrinsic to the probable origins of prosociality.
   (d) Authority and Respect. This presumably originated in the universal propensity for self-assertiveness, respect or humility being in some circumstances the best way to deal with the assertiveness of those in power.
   (e) Purity and sanctity. These are based on the emotion of disgust, and could have originated in basic propensities to avoid disease transmission[125] but also play a large part in religiously sponsored morality[47].

   Haidt and colleagues have found that, in several cultures, respondents who identify themselves as liberals tend to endorse especially the first two of these, whereas those who self-identify as conservatives tend to endorse all five. It is also the case that the last three especially have been endorsed especially by priests and others with an interest in promoting a religious system and thereby authenticating their positions. However, the view presented here suggests that the first three are all consequences of cultural group selection favouring groups whose members helped each other and thereby promoted the success of the group in competition with other groups. Authority and Respect is related to the survival of a group embedded in a potentially hostile environment or to the behaviour of individuals within a group with an hierarchical organisation. According to Haidt et al., the fifth category, Purity and Sanctity, is peculiar to humans and closely related to religion.
3. I use the term 'anti-theist' for those who seem to be actively opposed to religion, to contrast them with those atheists who believe there is no god

Notes

but do not find it necessary to spread their beliefs.
4. It is probable that the term 'neighbour' in the 10th Commandment referred also to Commandments 6 to 9. The admonition in Exodus 22, 21 often taken to imply 'foreigners' is diluted in Leviticus 19, 33 to strangers living locally. This is probably a translation error: the original uses the same word in both places (J. Emerton, pers. comm.). This is important because all groups have made a distinction between in-group and out-group.
5. For discussion of exceptions, see Hinde[84].
6. The literature on religion is almost infinite, and some recent debate has centred round the question of whether it is biologically adaptive. An important series of essays, with both sides of the debate, is given by Schloss & Murray[130]. It is not necessary to pursue the question of whether or not religion is *biologically* adaptive here. More important is the question of whether cultural selection has played a part in its evolution and radiation. It will be apparent that the present account of the evolution of morality is given in terms of cultural selection[27]. A classic example of the operation of cultural selection in the evolution of religion is given by D.S.Wilson's[167] account of how corruption in the Catholic Church led Calvin to propose a code of conduct which led to the reduction of factionalism in Geneva and other cities. Armstrong[6] has given another example from Muhammad's life.
7. Here and elsewhere I am not making a clear distinction between genetic and cultural selection. All human characteristics depend on both nature and nurture, though to varying degrees. Even those that seem quite ubiquitous, like the knee-jerk reflex, depend on the environment (pre- and post-natally) being within certain limits. Some aspects of behaviour, such as parental behaviour to one's own offspring, were certainly originally initiated by natural selection but have become a moral rule in human societies. It may make sense to talk of differences between individuals being due to genetic or environmental differences, but not of characteristics being one or the other. Even 'human nature' must be discussed in relation to the physical and social environment: differences over time may be related to genetic or socio-cultural changes. See Bateson & Gluckman[18].
8. The extent to which moral development is related to general skills of cognitive reasoning, the extent to which the development of the ideas of morality and convention are distinct in development, or depends on the rewards and punishments received in infancy, is controversial. A review is given by Schweder et al.,[131].
9. The concept of the 'environment of evolutionary adaptedness' was originally coined to refer to those features of the environment that are relevant to all infant humans, such as support against gravity or a nipple or nipple-shaped object to suck: the comment that the environments in which infants develop differ in many other respects is based on a misunderstanding of the scope of the concept.

10. Formal education developed in an era of families with multiple births where all except the more privileged classes had more opportunities for learning parenting skills than is the case today.
11. To avoid confusion, the European Convention for the Protection of Human Rights and Fundamental Freedoms (1950) is concerned solely with the duties of States to ensure that they observe and recognise the Rights of citizens as set out in the UN Declaration.

    The association between rights and duties is not emphasized in the 'Cairo Declaration on Human Rights in Islam' (Aug 5th, 1990). The Cairo Declaration on Human Rights in Islam, agreed at a meeting of Foreign Ministers in 1990, is based on Shari'ah Law and is also primarily for the guidance of states.
12. The concept of 'Social Capital', though clearly of great importance, has defied generally accepted definition: Putnam gives 'The nature and extent of networks and associated norms of reciprocity'. It has been divided into 'Bonding Social Capital' referring to trusting and cooperative relations between members of a network who see themselves as similar; 'Bridging Social Capital', involving relations of respect and mutuality between people who see themselves as different in age, ethnicity, social class and so on; and 'Linking Social Capital' involving individuals relating across formal or institutional power gradients in the society. All these types of social capital generally contribute to the cohesiveness of the society, but can also involve disruptive elements. See Szreter[145] for discussion.

References

1. Adams, H, (1876). Essays on Anglo-Saxon Law. Boston MA: Little Brown.
2. Ainsworth, M.D.S., Blehan,M.C., Waters,E. & Wall,S (1974). Patterns of Attachment. Hillsdale NJ: Erlbaum.
3. Alexander, R.D. (1987), The Biology of Moral Systems. New York: Aldine de Gruyter.
4. Allport, G.W. & Ross, J.M. (1967). Personal religion: orientation and prejudice. J. Personality & Social Psychology, 5, 432-43.
5. Appiah, K.A. (2010). The Honor Code. New York: Norton.
6. Armstrong, K. (1991). Muhammad: A Western Attempt to understand Islam. London: Victor Gollanz.
7. Armstrong, K. (2009). The Case for God: what Religion really means. London: Bodley Head.
8. Armstrong, K. (2010). Twelve steps to a compassionate life. London: Bodley Head.
9. Atran, S (2010). Talking to the enemy. London: Allen Lane (Penguin).
10. Atran, S. & Henrich, J. (2010). The evolution of religion. Biological Theory, 5, 18-30.
11. Backman, C.W. (1988). The Self: a dialectical approach. Advances in Experimental Psychology, 21, 229-260.
12. Bakermans-Kranenburg, M. J., & Van IJzendoorn, M.H. (2011). Differential susceptibility to rearing environment depending on dopamine-related genes: New evidence and a meta-analysis. Development and Psychopathology, 23, 39-52.
13. Bandura, A. (1997). Self-efficacy: the exercise of control. New York: Freeman.
14. Baron-Cohen, S. (1997). The Maladaptive Mind. Hove: Psychology Press.
15. Barrett, J. L. (2004). Why would Anyone Believe in God? Walnut Creek CA: AltaMira.
16. Barrett, J.L. (2009). Cognitive science, religion and theology. In Schloss & Murray, (Eds) (2009). The Believing Primate.
17. Bateson, M., Nettle, D. & Roberts, G. (2006). Cues of being watched enhance cooperation in a real world setting. Biological Letters (Royal Society), 2, 412-4.
18. Bateson, P & Gluckman, P. (2011). Plasticity, Robustness, Development & Evolution. Cambridge: Cambridge University Press.
19. Blair, R.J. (1997). A cognitive developmental approach to morality. In S. Baron-Cohn (ed.) The maladapted Mind. Hove: Psychology Press.
20. Blau, P.M. (1964). Exchange and Power in Social Life. New York: Wiley.
21. Boehm, C. (1991). Hierarchy in the Forest. Cambridge MA: Harvard University Press.
22. Botsman, R. & Rogers, R. (2011). What's Mine is Yours. London: Collins.
23. Bottéro, J. (1992). Mesopotamia: writing, reasoning and the gods.

24. Bowlby, J.(1969/1982, 1973, 1980). Attachment and Loss vol 1. Attachment; Vol 2 Separation: Anxiety and Anger; Vol 3 Loss: Sadness and Depression. London: Hogarth Press.
25. Bowles, S., Smith, E,A, & Borgerhof Mulder, M. (2010). Current Anthropology, 51, 7-17. (See also succeeding papers).
26. Boyd, R & Richerson, P. (1992). Punishment allows evolution of cooperation (or anything else) in sizeable groups. Ethology and Sociobiology, 13, 171-95.
27. Boyd, R. & Richerson, P. (2005). The Origin and Evolution of Cultures. Oxford: Oxford University Press.
28. Boyer, P. (1994). The Naturalness of Religious Ideas. Berkeley CA: University of California Press.
29. Boyer, P. (2001). Religion explained. New Haven: Basic Books.
30. Byrne, D. Nelson D, & Reenes, K. (1966). Effects of consensual validation and invalidation as a function of verifiability. J. Social and Experimental Psychology, 2, 98-107.
31. Cassidy, J. & Shaver, P.R., Eds. (2008). Handbook of attachment, 2nd Ed.: Theory, research, and clinical applications. New York: Guilford Press.
32. Catholic Bishops Conference of England and Wales. (undated). The Common Good. London: The Catholic Bishops Conference.
33. Chen, X (2011). Culture and children's socioemotional functioning: a contextual-development perspective. In Chen & Rubin, eds. 2011.
34. Chen, X. & Rubin, K. (2011)(eds.). Socioemotional Development in Cultural Context. New York: Guilford Press.
35. Clutton-Brock, T. (2009). Cooperation between non-kin in animal societies. Nature, 462/5, 51-57.
36. Cohen, R. (2011). Religion does its worst. NY Times, April 5.
37. Colby, A. & Damon, W.(1995). The development of extraordinary moral commitment. In M. Killen & D. Hart (eds). Morality in Everyday Life. Cambridge: Cambridge University Press.
38. Darley, J. & Batson, C.D. (1973). From Jerusalem to Jericho: a study of situational and dispositional variables in helping behavior. J. Pers. Soc. Psychol., 27, 100-08.
39. Dasgupta, P. (2001). Human well-being and the natural environment. Oxford: Oxford University Press.
40. Dasgupta, P. (2009). Trust and cooperation among economic agents, Phil. Trans. Royal Society, 364, 3301-09.
41. Dawkins, R. (2006). The God Delusion. London: Transworld.
42. Dennett, D.C. (2006). Breaking the evil spell: religion as a natural phenomenon. London: Viking.
43. Des Pres, T. (1976). The survivor: an anatomy of life in the death camps. Oxford University Press: New York.

References

44. De Wolff, M.S. & van IJzendoorn, M.H. (1997). Sensitivity and attachment. Child Development, 688, 571-91.
45. Dormor, D. (2004). Just Cohabiting. London: Darton, Longman & Todd.
46. Dormor, D. (2008). Science as a Moral Endeavour. Sermon delivered in St. John's College Chapel, Cambridge, 23 November, 2008.
47. Douglas, M. (1970). Purity and Danger. Harmondsworth: Penguin.
48. Drescher (2011), Antislavery debates. European Review, 19, 131-48.
49. Dudbridge, G. (1995) Religious Experience and Lay Society in T'ang China. Cambridge: Cambridge University Press.
50. Dunbar, R. (1996). Grooming, Gossip and the Evolution of Language. London: Faber and Faber.
51. Dunbar, R. (2004). The Human Story. London: Faber & Faber.
52. Durkheim, E. (1951). Suicide. New York: Free Press.
53. Eagleton, T. (2009). Reason, Faith and Revolution. New Haven CA: Yale University Press.
54. Edwards, C.P (2000). Children's play in cross-cultural perspective. Cross-Cultural Research, 34, 318-38.
55. Ekman, P. (1985). Telling Lies. New York: Norton.
56. Elsdon-Baker, E. (2009). The Selfish Genius. London: Icon Books.
57. Erdal, D. & Whiten, A. (1996). Egalitarianism and Machiavellian intelligence in human evolution. In Mellars, P. and Gibson, K (eds.), Modelling the early Human Mind, p. 139-50. Cambridge: McDonald Institute.
58. Evans-Pritchard, E.E. (1951). Some features of Nuer religion. J. Royal Anthropological Institute, 81, 1-14.
59. Evans-Wentz, W.Y. (ed.) (1957). The Tibetan Book of the Dead. New York: Oxford University Press.
60. Fachler,M. (2011). New York Times, March 23 2011.
61. Farver, J.M., Kim, Y.K. & Lee, Y. (1995). Cultural differences in Korean and Anglo-American preschoolers' social interaction and play behaviours. Child Development, 66, 1088-99.
62. Fehr, E. & Fischbacher, U. (2003). The nature of human altruism. Nature, 425, 785-91.
63. Gambetta, D. (1988). Can we trust? In D. Gambetta (ed.) Trust. Oxford: Blackwell.
64. Gelman, R., Durgin, F., & Kaufman, L. (1995). Distinguishing between animates and inanimates: not by motion alone. In D. Sperber, D. Premack and D.J. Premack (eds). Causal Cognition. Oxford: Clarendon.
65. Gilligan, C. (1983). In a different voice, Cambridge MA: Harvard University Press.
66. Goody, E. (1991). The learning of prosocial behaviour in small-scale egalitarian societies. In Hinde, R.A. & Groebel, J. (eds.) Cooperation and Prosocial Behaviour. Cambridge: Cambridge University Press.

67. Granqvist, P. & Hagekull, B. (1999). Religiousness and perceived attachment. J. Scientific Study of Religion, 38, 254-73.
68. Graves, N.R. & Graves, T.D. (1983). The cultural context of prosocial development. In D.L.Bridgeman (ed.) The Nature of Prosocial Development. San Diego CA: Academic Press.
69. Guidi, M.G.D., Hillier, J. & Tarbert, H. (2010). Successfully reshaping the ownership relationship by reducing 'Moral debt' and justly redistributing the residual claims. Critical Accounting, 21, 318-28.
70. Guthrie, S. (1993). Faces in the clouds. New York: Oxford University Press.
71. Hackney, C.H. & Sanders, G.S. (2003). Religiosity and mental health. J. Scientific Study of Religion, 42, 43-55.
72. Haidt, J. (2009). Moral Psychology and the misunderstanding of religion. In Schloss & Murray.
73. Hamilton, W.D. (1964) The genetical evolution of social behavior. J. Theoretical Biology, 7, 1-52.
74. Hannay, D.R. (1980). Religion and health. Social Science and Medicine, 14, 683-85.
75. Haslam, S.A. & Reicher, S.D. (2007). Beyond the banality of evil. Personality & Social Psychology Bulletin 33, 615-22.
76. Hauser, M. (2006). Moral Minds. New York: Ecco.
77. Hauser, M., McAuliffe, K. & Blake, P.R. (2009). Evolving the ingredients for reciprocity and spite. Philosophical Trans. Royal Society, 364, 3255-66.
78. Henrich, J. (2009). The evolution of costly displays, cooperation and religion. Evolution and Human Behavior, 30. 244-60.
79. Henrich, J. & Boyd, R. (2001). Why people punish defectors. J. Theoretical Biology, 208, 79-89.
80. Henrich, J., Boyd, R. & 15 others. (2005). 'Economic Man' in cross-cultural perspective. Behavioral and Brain Sci 28,795-855.
81. Hewlett, B.S., Fouts, H.N. Boyette, A.H. & Hewlett B.L.(2011). Social learning among Congo Basin hunter-gatherers. In Whiten et al., (eds) (2011). Culture evolves. Phil. Trans. Roy. Soc. B. 366, 1168-78.
82. Hill, K. & Hurtado, M. (1996). Aché life-history: the ecology and demography of a foraging people. Hawthorne NY: Aldine de Gruyter.
83. Hinde, R.A. (1997). Relationships: a Dialectical Perspective. Hove: Psychology Press.
84. Hinde, R,A, (2002). Why Good is Good. London: Routledge.
85. Hinde, R.A. (2006). Ending War. Nottingham: Spokesman.
86. Hinde, R.A. (2007). Bending the Rules. Oxford: Oxford University Press.
88. Hinde, R.A. (2010). Why Gods Persist (2nd ed). London: Routledge.
89. Hinde, R.A. (2011). Society needs morality. European Review, 19, 105-118.
90. Hinde, R.A. & Rotblat, J. (2003). War No More. London: Pluto.

References

91. Hinde, R.A. & Stevenson-Hinde, J.S. (1973). Constraints on Learning. London: Academic Press.
92. Hitchens, C. (2007). God is not Great. London: Atlantic.
93. Hobsbawm, J. (ed.) (2006). Where the Truth Lies. London: Atlantic.
94. Hoffman, E. & Spitzer, M. (1985). Entitlements, rights and fairness. Journal of Legal Studies, 14, 259-97.
95. Holloway, R. (1999). Godless Morality. Edinburgh: Canongate.
96. Homans, G.C. (1961). Social Behavior: its elementary Forms. London, Routledge, Kegan Paul.
97. Hrdy, S. (1999). Mother Nature. New York: Pantheon.
98. Hutton, W. (2010). Them and Us. London: Little, Brown.
99. Iannacone, L.R. (1995). Why strict churches are strong, American J. of Sociology, 99, 1180-211.
100. James, O. (2008). The Selfish Capitalist. London: Vermillion.
101. Johnson, D. & Bering, J. (2009). Hand of God, mind of man. In Schloss & Murray (2009).
102. Johnson, P. (1995) The Withered Garland. London: New European Publications.
103. Kaplan, H. & Hill, K. (1985). Hunting ability and reproductive success among male Aché foragers. Current Anthropology. 26, 131-3.
104. Koenig H.G., McCullough, M.E. & Larson, D.B. (2001). Handbook of Religion and Health. Oxford: Oxford University Press.
105. Kohn, M. (2008). Trust: Self-interest and the Common Good. Oxford: Oxford University Press.
106. Konner, M. (2010). The Evolution of Childhood: relationships, emotion, mind. Cambridge, Mass.: Harvard University Press.
107. Krugman, P. (2009). The Conscience of a Liberal. London: Penguin.
108. Küng, H. & Kuschel, L. (1993). A global Ethic. London: SCM Press.
109. Lloyd, G.E.R. (2004). Ancient Worlds, Modern Reflections. Oxford: Oxford University Press.
110. Lott, T, (2010). Father, I have sinned – I'm an atheist. Times, Dec. 13, 2010.
111. Macfarlane, A. (1978). The Origins of English Individualism. Oxford: Blackwell.
112. Macfarlane, A. (2008). Japan, through the looking glass. London: Profile Books.
113. McGuire, W.J. & McGuire, C.V. (1988). Content and process in the experience of self. Advances in Experimental Social Psychology, 21, 97-44.
114. McKay, R., Efferson, C. Whitehouse, H. & Fehr, E. (2011). Wrath of God: religious primes and punishment. Proc. Roy. Soc. B, 278, 1858-63.
115. Midgley, M. (1994). The Ethical Primate. London: Routledge.
116. Norenzayan, A. & Shariff, A.F. (2008). The origin and evolution of

religious prosociality. Science, 322, 58-62.
117. Norenzayan, A., Smith, E.E., Kim, B.J. & Nisbett, R.E. (2002). Cultural preferences for formal versus intuitive reasoning. Cognitive Science, 26, 653-84.
118. Norman, R. (2004) On Humanism. London: Routledge.
119. Nucci, L. & Lee, J. (1993). Morality and personal autonomy. In G.G.Noam & T.E.Wran (eds) The Moral Self. Cambridge MA: MIT Press.
120. O'Keefe, J. (1996). I'll tell you a secret. An introduction to Catholic social teaching. Catholic Agency for Overseas Devlopment.
121. Petrinovich, L. (1997). Human evolution, reproduction and morality. New York: Plenum.
122. Putnam, R. (2000). Bowling Alone: the Collapse and Revival of American Community. Cambridge, Mass: Harvard University Press.
123. Randolph-Seng, B. & Nielsen, M.E. (2007). Honesty: one effect of primed religious representations. International J. Psychology Religion, 17, 303-15.
124. Roemer, J.E. (1996). Egalitarian Perspectives. Cambridge: Cambridge University Press.
125. Rozin, P. & Nemeroff, C. (1990). The laws of sympathetic magic. In Stigler et al., (eds) (1990).
126. Runciman, D, (2008). Political Hypocrisy. Princeton NJ: Princeton University Press.
127. Sands, P. (2008). Torture team: Deception, cruelty and the Compromise of Law. Allen Lane.
128. Santos, M. dos, Rankin, D.J. & Wedkind, C. (2011). The Evolution of punishment through reputation. Proc. Roy Soc. B., 278, 371-377.
129. Scheper-Hughes, N. (1992). Death without Weeping: the Violence of everyday Life in Brazil. Berkeley, CA: University of California Press.
130. Schloss, J. & Murray, M. (eds) (2009). The Believing Primate. Oxford: Oxford University Press.
131. Schweder, R.A., Mahapatra, M. & Miller, J.G. (1990). Culture and moral development. In Stigler et al., (eds)(1990).
132. Seligman, M.E.P & Hager, J.L (1972). Biological Boundaries of Learning, New York: Appleton Century Crofts.
133. Shakson, N. (2011). Treasure Islands. London: Bodley Head.
134. Sharf, R.H. (1966). The scripture in 42 sections. In D.S. Lopez (ed.) Religions of China in practice, Princeton, NJ: Princeton University Press.
135. Shariff, A.F. & Norenzayan, A. (2007). God is watching you: priming god concepts in an anonymous economic game. Psychological Science, 18, 803-09.
136. Shklar, J. N. (1984) Ordinary Vices. Cambridge Mass: Harvard University Press.

References

137. Sims, A. & Boyle, D. (2010). Eminent Corporations. London: Constable.
138. Sosis, R. & Bressler, E.R. (2003). Cooperation and commune longevity: a test of the costly signalling theory of religion. Cross-cultural Research, 37, 211-39.
139. Stark, R. & Glock, G.C. (1968). American Piety: the nature of religious commitment. Berkeley CA; University of California Press.
140. Stevenson-Hinde, J. (2011). Culture and socio-emotional development, with a focus on fearfulness and attachment. In Chen & Rubin, (eds.) Socioemotional Development in Cultural Context.
141. Stevenson-Hinde, J., Shouldice, A. & Chicot, R. (2011). Maternal anxiety, behavioural inhibition and attachment. Attachment and Human Development, 13, 199-216.
142. Stigler, J.W., Schweder, R.A. & Herdt, A. (eds.)(1990). Cultural Psychology. Cambridge: Cambridge University Press.
143. Stiglitz, J. (2006). Making Globalization work. London: Penguin.
144. Sunstein, C.A. (2005). Moral heuristics. Behavioral and Brain Sciences, 28, 531- 573.
145. Szreter, S. (2005). Health by association? Social capital, social theory and the public economy of public health. In S. Szreter (ed.) Health and Wealth. Rochester NY: University of Rochester Press.
146. Szreter, S, 2010. The WHO and the Social Determinants of Health Report 2008. In S. Bhattacharya, S. Messenger & C. Overy (eds.) Social Determinants of Health. Hyderabad: Orint Black Swan.
147. Szreter, S. & Fisher, K. (2010). Sex before the Sexual Revolution. Cambridge: Cambridge University Press.
148. Tomasello, M. (2009). Why we cooperate. Cambridge, MASS: MIT Press.
149. Toynbee, P. (2010). There's no such thing as an ethical Tory. Saturday Guardian, Feb. 20, 2010.
150. Toynbee, P. & Walker, D. (2008). Unjust Rewards. London: Granta.
151. Tremlin, T (2005). Divergent Religion: a dual process model of religious thought, behavior and morphology. In H. Whitehouse & R.N. McCauley (eds.) Mind and Religion. Walnut Creek CA: AltaMira.
152. Triandis, H,C, (1991). Cross-cultural differences in assertiveness/competitiveness vs group loyalty/cooperation. In R.A.Hinde & J. Grobel (eds) Cooperation and Prosocial Behaviour. Cambridge: Cambridge University Press.
153. Trivers, R. (1974). Parent–infant conflict. American Zoologist,14, 249-64.
154. Trivers, R. (1985) Social Evolution. Menlo Park CA: Benjamin/Cummings.
155. Turiel, E. (1983). The development of social knowledge: morality and convention. Cambridge: Cambridge University Press.
156. Turiel, E. (1998). The development of social knowledge. In W. Damon & N. Eisenberg (eds.) Handbook of Child Psychology, 5th Edition. New York: Wiley.

157. Uslaner, E. (2002). The Moral Foundations of Trust. Cambridge: Cambridge University Press.
158. van IJzendoorn, M.H. & Sagi, A. (2008). Cross-cultural paterns of attachment: universal and contextual dimensions. In Cassidy & Shaver (eds)
159. Vidler, A.R. (1964). Historical objections, In D.M.Mackinnon, H.A.Williams, A.R.Vidler & J.S.Bezzant (eds). Objections to Christian belief. London: Constable.
160. Wainryb, C. (1993). The application of moral judgements to other cultures. Child Development, 64, 924-33.
161. Whitehouse, H. (2000). Arguments and Icons: Divergent Modes of Religiosity. Oxford: Oxford University Press.
162. Whiten, A. (1994). On human egalitarianism. Current Anthropology, 35, 175-183.
163. Whiten, A., Hinde, R.A., Stringer, C.B. & Laland K. (eds) (2011). Culture evolves. Phil. Trans. Royal Soc. B, 366, 935-1187.
164. Wilkinson, R. & Pickett, K. (2009). The Spirit Level. London: Penguin.
165. Williams, B. (1985). Ethics and the limits of Philosophy. London: Fontana.
166. Williams, R, (2010) Empathy, not individuality, is key to humanity. Guardian Feb 2 2010, p.10.
167. Wilson, D.S, (2002). Darwin's Cathedral: Evolution, Religion and the Nature of Society. Chicago ILL: University of Chicago Press.
168. Wilson, D.S, (2009). Evolutionary Social Constructivism. (and other contributions in Schloss & Murray (2009).